I0471744

More Money For Pensioners!

How to Survive Retirement on a Lousy State Pension & Claim All Your OAP Benefits & Entitlements

Martin Woodward

ISBN 978-1-291-86948-4

Copyright © Martin Woodward 2014

All rights reserved

Enquiries: http://martinwoodward.net

*This book has been written for you with only **your** best interests in mind!*

Acknowledgements

Grateful thanks go to friend Alan Simonds for his help and advice - thanks Alan. And also to friend and next door neighbour Mike Taylor for the same - thanks Mike.

Contents

Introduction

Congratulations, you've made it to retirement without snuffing it! Now you want to enjoy what time you've got left on this planet. And there's no reason why your remaining years shouldn't be your best of your life - regardless of your income.

It perhaps seems a little unfair, but having reached this point we are all on different incomes.

You will no doubt come into one of the following categories:

- Basic pension with no other pensions, savings / investments or earnings;

- Basic pension plus other pensions and / or savings;

- Basic pension plus gold plated index linked public sector pension with or without additional savings.

Additional variations could be that:

- If you've worked for an employer your basic pension will be topped up with the 'SERPS' payment;

- You own your own property;

- You live in a rented council property;

- You could be property rich and income poor or property poor and income rich.

So clearly we all have different situations and vastly different living expenses and incomes. But the one thing that we have in common is that we're all on a lower income than we're used to and we're all becoming gradually more vulnerable.

But even if you are on the lowest basic pension with no savings and live in a council property, fear not - you live in the land of Milk and Honey which you should be very thankful for. And the worse your situation, the more you will need to apply the information herein.

The object here is to help you get the best out of your individual circumstances.

And of course your circumstances could change radically overnight due to the death of a spouse (or divorce), where the remaining partner could be left with a greatly reduced income and the same high utility bills. So even if this information is inapplicable to you right now, it might not be in the future.

So how come you know so much?

Well, I've been round the block a few times. I've been self employed virtually all of my life including back in the days when there were no benefits for self employed people, however much they didn't have.

I've been unemployed and penniless numerous times (and not claimed any benefits), but I've also fought back and enjoyed my own luxury Villa in Cyprus, with pool and all the trimmings.

And like you I am a pensioner - and now back in the UK.

Apart from all this - *my wife knows everything! She's a walking talking encyclopaedia that never shuts up!* So if I need to know anything, I just ask her! But she always tells me everything she thinks I need to know before I even think of it anyway!

Those Who Have Least Pay Most

It's a sad fact that the poorest in society pay most for just about everything.

Why?

Because:

- They don't have any extra contingency funds in order to take advantage of BOGOF'S or bulk buys of genuine short term half price offers;

- They're the most likely to get screwed by the banks for going overdrawn etc.;

- They often fall foul of payday loans just to 'survive';

- They are often forced to use higher priced prepayment meters for utilities;

- They often smoke or drink (or take drugs) or gamble when they clearly can't afford to;

- They're often incapable of or unwilling to help themselves by budgeting correctly and / or looking into the full range of benefits available to them. However, often in the case of single parents, they *do* have sufficient funds given to them, they just mismanage them through ignorance - kids having kids;

- They may be mentally subnormal, which is certainly a crime where society allows such individuals to be penalized through no fault of their own.

The above applies to all poor, young and old, and the information here could help both, but has primarily been written with pensioners in mind.

Let's face it you and I both come from an era when it was considered shameful to accept any form of charity, social benefits or to go bankrupt. And quite possibly you've never claimed any social benefit all your life and have no idea about claiming it or whether you are entitled to anything more than your basic state pension. Whereas the younger generations often see benefits as a way of life and an automatic continual entitlement even though they may have paid little or nothing into it.

But we've paid our whack and you must remember that any benefits that you are genuinely entitled to are **your right** which **you** have paid for. So don't feel bad about taking them and you may be surprised at what you actually **are** entitled to.

What the Dickens?

As you're from the same generation as me, you'll possibly remember the following quotation:

"Annual income twenty pounds, annual expenditure nineteen pounds nineteen and six, result happiness. Annual income twenty pounds, annual expenditure twenty pounds nought and six, result misery." Mr Micawber - David Copperfield - Charles Dickens.

Put very simply this means that you should live within your means, whatever your income happens to be.

No-one would deny that this is good, sound advice for individuals, households, businesses and governments and you would think that even the dumbest of the dumb would follow it. Yet many don't, particularly the young and fool hardy and surprisingly many businesses and governments (I'm not going to get political here, so I'm not saying which).

In the case of individuals, this is stupid, in the case of businesses - wishful thinking or planned bankruptcy and in the case of governments - an unforgiveable disgrace!

Now I'm going to show you a possibly typical but hypothetical example of a pension nightmare.

This example is for a couple on the very basic state pension with a very small private pension. As you can see this equates to £209.75 per week including the annual fuel allowance which may or may not continue.

Mr & Mrs Not-So-Clever Income		
	Weekly	Monthly
State Pension	£180.90	£783.90
Private Pension	£25.00	£108.33
Winter Fuel Allnce	£3.85	£16.67
Total Income	**£209.75**	**£908.90**

Then we add the expenses below, and note that this couple own their property freehold and therefore have no rent to pay. Neither are they in debt - although clearly they will be soon.

Mr & Mrs Not-So-Clever Expenditure		
	Weekly	Monthly
Rent / Mortgage	£0.00	£0.00
Council Tax	£25.51	£110.54
Heat / Light	£25.00	£108.33
Water	£10.00	£43.33
Groceries	£94.40	£409.07
Telephone / Internet	£10.00	£43.33
TV Licence	£2.50	£10.83
White Goods Insurance	£4.00	£17.33
Loans / Debts	£0.00	£0.00
White Goods Replacement	£3.00	£13.00
Motoring	£57.00	£247.00
Clothes	£20.00	£86.67
Xmas	£20.00	£86.67
Window cleaner	£2.50	£10.83
Incidental	£10.00	£43.33
Holidays	£25.00	£108.33
Emergency Repairs	£10.00	£43.33
Entertainment	£20.00	£86.67
Dental / Optical	£2.00	£8.67
Life Insurance	£5.00	£21.67
Pet Insurance	£4.00	£17.33
House Insurance	£4.00	£17.33
Total	£353.91	£1,533.61

Now we'll look at the balance below, and as you can see this is an unsustainable disaster which would no doubt make Mr Micawber turn in his fictional grave.

Mr & Mrs Not-So-Clever Balance		
	Weekly	**Monthly**
Total Income	£209.75	£908.90
Total Expenditure	£353.91	£1,533.61
Balance	-£144.16	-£624.71

Obviously, this example is extreme and totally unsustainable, but shortly I will show you how to fix this through a combination of increasing income and reducing outgoings.

Knowledge is power

But to begin with, don't try to change anything, just find out exactly how things are by closely scrutinising every aspect of your income and expenditure - *honestly* - don't leave anything out - and don't forget the items that are only paid out once a year.

Then we'll start looking at what can be altered to either increase your income and / or reduce your expenditure.

It's a balancing act that will either cause contentment or misery.

Now if you have a PC you can download copies of the excel spreadsheets just shown which will allow you to alter the figures and add or change various items to suit your circumstances. See: http://martinwoodward.net/pen1.html .

Note that the areas marked in light blue (or grey if seen in black and white) cannot be altered and to edit the groceries and motoring items you will have to go to sheet 2. The results will be updated automatically.

If you don't have a computer, you will have to do this on paper which of course is more time consuming.

All of the hyperlinks shown throughout this book are also listed in the Resources section at the end which can be downloaded separately making it easy to gain access to all of the links especially if you have the printed version.

See: http://martinwoodward.net/resources.html .

Become Computer Savvy

Quite possibly you are already, in which case great!

Well, I'm not so why should I be?

A few years ago it wasn't essential to have a bank account as you will no doubt remember - when we all got paid in cash at the end of the week. But just as bank accounts have become essential, it's only a matter of time before an internet connection will become essential for various reasons.

I'd like to bet that this will be the case within ten years. So now is the time to learn all this stuff, while you've still got your marbles. And actually learning it is good for your marbles and could open up a whole new world of interest and knowledge to you as well as saving you money, far over and above the cost of purchasing a basic PC.

In brief a PC (personal computer or laptop) can be used for:

- Internet Banking;
- Online Shopping (for just about anything);
- Searching out the best price for insurances and utilities;
- Surfing the web for information;
- Downloading and watching videos;
- Downloading valuable money saving vouchers;
- Keeping account of your household spending easily;
- Keeping in touch with friends and family via *free* Skype video calls;
- Writing letters.

And the above is just the beginning. In addition to all of these I also use mine for:

- Writing and publishing my books;

- Writing and recording music;
- Creating websites;
- Creating You Tube videos;
- Storing photographs.

If you ever become in the situation where you can't get out, or transport becomes a problem, then you could order groceries (plus just about everything else) online. Actually, when you think about the time and effort involved, this is a very cost effective way of shopping.

But if you really don't want to get involved in computers, it's not *absolutely* essential for what we're doing here, but you would find it very helpful, especially as many of the examples I will be giving here will also be available as downloadable excel files that you can play around with.

Now the object of this book is not to teach you how to use a computer, but I will give you a few pointers, although if you've never used a computer before I strongly recommend that you get the 'Which' guide for computer beginners and preferably also get some help and advice from friends or relatives.

So what sort of computer do I need and how much do they cost?

Well if you just want the very bare minimum, I would suggest either a laptop or netbook.

So what's the difference?

Well mainly speed, power and storage. I use a Toshiba Laptop with a 500 gigabyte hard drive and 8 gig of RAM with a fairly fast CPU which uses Windows 8. This cost me £330 from Argos and does everything that I want it to. A new netbook could cost less than £200.

You've lost me.

Ok, the bigger the Hard Drive (HD), the more programs and information you will be able to store on the computer. The RAM is the working memory used by the programs and the more RAM you have, the faster the PC will work especially if opening more than one program at a time. The CPU is the engine that makes it all work. Windows 8 is the latest operating system.

My last PC had a 160 gig hard drive, 3 gig of RAM, a less powerful CPU and ran on Windows Vista operating system. Even that (which is now outdated) worked for me, although I was struggling for memory on my music files, but this would easily be more than enough as a starter computer.

What's a program?

A program is an application often referred to as an 'app'.

When you first get a computer, if no programs are installed all you would be able to do is surf the web.

Initially the most important programs that a beginner would want to install are:

- MS Excel (spreadsheet for calculations);
- MS Word for letter writing;
- Skype for making and receiving *free* video calls with friends;
- An anti virus programme such as MS Security Essentials.

When buying a new PC it will almost certainly come with a trial version of an anti virus programme such as Norton or McAfee in the hope that you buy the full version. But you don't need either of these as MS Security Essentials is fine and free.

You would need to buy and install Excel and Word, but you don't particularly need the latest (and most expensive version) Office 2007 contains these and is widely economically available. Or alternatively you could use one of the free suites such as libreoffice which can be downloaded free at http://www.libreoffice.org/download .

If you want to get onto the web, you would need an internet provider (usually but not necessarily through your phone line). Costs for this can vary considerably, so you will need to do some homework. I use Plusnet for phone and internet, who are ok.

You would also need to register a free email address typically with Google, Hotmail or Yahoo. Having done this, write it down along with the password so that you don't forget it.

Google is a good place to have an email address, which is free incidentally and fairly safe as they filter out a certain amount of the bad stuff.

But beyond all this there are thousands of other programs which you may like to install and use. For instance I use:

- Serif webplus 6 - for creating websites;
- Serif Moviemaker - for making YouTube videos;
- Serif Pageplus and Corel Draw for creating graphics;
- Melody Assistant - for creating music notation;
- Cakewalk Sonar X2 - for recording music;
- Plus many more.

But each time you install a new program, to a certain extent it's like starting all over again - you have to learn the functions of the particular programs. Some are very easy while others take months - even for an veteran.

Online Storage

It's always a good idea to back up (save) important files (and photos) onto an external hard drive, just in case your PC or laptop ever needs reformatting through a virus etc. External hard drives are available for about £50.

As an alternative (or as well as) you could use online storage such as Google Drive & Sky Drive. Both of these offer up to 5GB of free online storage. I use both and have to say that they've saved me the inconvenience of having to commit suicide on a number of occasions.

Photobucket or Snapfish are good free places to store and edit your photos online. For further info see http://photobucket.com and http://www.snapfish.com .

Smart TVs

At sometime in the future you will almost certainly get involved with a smart TV, which are the latest generation of TVs currently not owned by the masses. But give it a couple of years and more or less everyone will have one. The main function of these is to enable free 'catch up TV' which is achieved via internet 'streaming' and as such requires an unlimited broadband connection.

Your existing TV can be converted to a smart TV by connecting an XBMC smart TV box. These are available on eBay for about £50 (but you must have an unlimited broadband with at least an average download speed).

Social Network Site

The two most popular social networking sites are Facebook and Twitter and there's clearly no doubt that they're very popular.

Personally I don't use either of them as all the friends I have are 'real' friends who I speak to face to face, over the telephone or on Skype. I don't need hundreds of imaginary Facebook friends. And I don't want to 'follow' anyone and I don't want anyone 'following' me as on Twitter, in fact I find the whole idea of it 'creepy'!

Twice my laptop has been infected with serious viruses (which I'll be talking about soon), and both originated from Facebook.

So if you do use these sites all I would say is, be vigilant and aware of the dangers.

eBay / Amazon / Paypal

Without doubt eBay and Amazon are the two leading online auction and selling sites.

As you probably know eBay can be used by private sellers as well as traders. If buying anything expensive from a private seller, I would advise collecting it from their home and making sure that it is legitimate before parting with cash. While there are buyer protection facilities in place for items bought from traders, there is no protection if you buy in cash from a private seller. Always check the sellers feedback and if it's not 95% positive, stay clear. And never arrange to meet anyone on a street corner carrying a wad of cash for obvious reasons! Buyer beware!

Amazon is slightly more upmarket than eBay and deals entirely with traders and not private sellers. Other online selling sites are shown in the resources section at the end.

Paypal is the payment facility owned by eBay but also used by many online traders (me included). In order to purchase something via Paypal, you can use your debit / credit card or open a Paypal account.

All of these sites are prime targets for 'phishing' (details in next section).

The Dark Side

As with everything good, there is also a dark side which you must be forever wary of. And newcomers are most likely to fall foul of them.

The worst of these are:

- Phishing;
- Viruses;
- Bogus emails (usually from Nigeria);
- Online Gaming;
- Pornography.

While internet banking is generally safe and secure you should make sure that you do not give your bank details out to anyone either deliberately or accidentally.

Unfortunately there are many individuals who send out bogus emails supposedly from your bank asking you to log on (unwittingly to them) for various reasons, then once they have your details, they also have access to your funds. These emails look very authentic, so you must be vigilant. I get literally hundreds of them. This is known as 'phishng' (fishing for your passwords etc.). When you find one of these emails, report them to the company who they are pretending to be from by 'forwarding' the message to the company.

A good rule of thumb is:

- Install a suitable antivirus program such as Microsoft Security Essentials (free) http://www.microsoft.com and an anti malware program such as Spybot at http://www.safer-networking.org (also free);

- Never log onto your bank via an email or when someone asks you to. Always enter their website and your account the normal way;

- Protect your accounts using the Trusteer Protection (free application from your bank);

- Only ever 'bank' online via a secure service provider. Or in other words not from a free wifi provider where anyone could be accessing your details;

- Always check the correct bank URL (website name) and that it starts with **https://** plus a little padlock - this is a secure site whereas most unsecure sites start with **http://** ;

- Change your passwords periodically and don't use the same ones for different banks etc.;

- If you think that your bank account or credit card has been compromised in anyway, contact your bank immediately - via telephone;

- When downloading *free* programs etc., watch out that you don't also unwittingly download any nasty little add-ons such as *Linkey*, *Babylon* or *Conduit etc.,* which creep around your computer gathering information about you. Many programmes are *free* just in order to dupe you into these nasties! Your antimalware programme should help prevent these.

Viruses are usually 'caught' by opening dodgy emails. Once your computer becomes infected, usually the only way to get rid of them is to wipe your hard drive and re-install the operating system, thereby losing everything that you have stored on the drive - hence the reason for backing up important files on an external hard drive.

Bogus emails (often from Nigeria although you wouldn't necessarily know this), usually suggest that you have just won some little known lottery (that you never entered) and need to send them a fee in order to receive the winnings. Or they may say that they've been given your name as someone they can trust in order to help them claim a legacy by paying it into your bank in exchange for a huge fee (of course they only want your bank details). Often they also pull at your heart strings with hard luck stories and bring 'God' into it. - Delete them all - I get thousands!

If you are a gambler with an addictive personality, online gambling (including Bingo) can very quickly wipe you away. It's advertised to look fun, but it's ruthless and is the ruin of many and often not even regulated so they may even be cheating!

Similarly, I guess that online pornography is there for anyone who happens to be looking for it and this is a particular worry for children to be exposed to. But unfortunately with new technology comes these new evils. Recently some search engines such as Google have agreed to disallow the worst of these. Personally I can't see why they ever allowed them in the first place.

So all in all you would be wise to get some help and advice certainly before attempting online banking.

Seek help from other OAPs or give help to others if you have the knowledge!

Increasing Your Income

If you are on a fixed pension, you probably think that increasing your income is impossible short of winning the lottery. Well, it may not be; but how you can achieve this, depends on your current income and personal circumstances.

The following options may be open to you:

- Pension Credit;
- Equity Release;
- Downsize;
- Cash back & Loyalty Cards;
- Part time work;
- Taking a lodger;
- Increasing returns on investments;
- Annuities;
- Rent out your garage;
- Dig for victory;
- Swap your skills.

Pension Credit

Pension credit is a means tested income related benefit made up of **'guaranteed credit'** and / or **'savings credit'**.

If your individual or joint income falls below the minimum amount set out by the government (currently £226.50 per week for couples and 148.35 for a single person), you may be able to claim the most important 'guaranteed' credit. But even if your income(s) is / are above these figures you may be able to claim the 'savings' credit.

However, after the first £10,000 of joint savings, any additional savings are considered to be income of £2.00 per week per thousand (10%). But even still a couple on the minimum basic joint pension of £180.90 per week could have savings of £32,500 and still be eligible for the guaranteed credit, which would also give them a whole host of other benefits, some of which are listed below:

- Free council tax;
- Ground rent payments;
- Rent payments;
- Additional winter fuel payments by registering for the Warm Home Discount Scheme;
- Free Dental Care;
- Free glasses (up to certain limits);
- Free chiropody;
- Boiler / insulation grants;
- Funeral grants;
- Free Pet Care (from the PDSA).

So for anyone who is income poor and property / investment rich, it might even be worth moving to a more expensive property (thus lowering capital) in order to become eligible for this valuable benefit.

Ironically if the hypothetical couple above had even £1 more savings which would put them in the £33,000 bracket (as it's calculated to £500 above) they would be substantially worse off, in the fact that they wouldn't receive all the additional benefits listed above (particularly 100% free council tax).

And what really annoys me is that, anyone thinking they may be eligible, may go through all the grief of filling out the official form only to be told that they aren't entitled to the guaranteed credit, but if they miss out by £1, they may not be informed of this.

Because of this I have created a very simple and quick calculator which shows you how far off you are. But note that this calculator **doesn't** show the savings credit which you may be entitled to anyway (up to a maximum of £28.89 per week) and if you own your own home, you may be entitled to this even if you don't have any savings. So it's worth looking into!

To download my free easy calculator go to http://martinwoodward.net/pen.html . After inputting your information, if a negative figure appears (in red), this means that you are not eligible for the guaranteed credit due to your current income and savings. But if this is the case play around with it for a bit by hypothetically reducing your savings to see how close you are.

But even if you are not eligible for the guaranteed credit you may be eligible for the savings credit and possibly a reduction in your council tax payments (if your savings are below £16k). To find this out easily, the next best calculator to use is the Age UK form which can be found at http://www.ageuk.org.uk/money-matters/claiming-benefits/pension-credit - click the 'online benefits calculator' half way down the page.

If you find that you are eligible, then make the calculations again (which takes longer) on the official form at https://www.gov.uk/pension-credit and then make your application by phone at 0800 99 1234. Note that you may have to apply for council tax rebates / discounts directly from your council, but deal with the pension credit first.

The DWP will need to see evidence of your income and savings (bank statements etc.) before approving your claim.

Millions of pounds are going unclaimed. The government know this and keep advertising the fact, but from their point of view they'd probably prefer you to die quickly of hypothermia, then you'd save them a fortune!

I know and they know that it's not in the makeup of our generation to claim benefits. But you've paid for it, it's your entitlement - TAKE IT! You could be just one luxury cruise away from a higher income which I'll show you later!

Both elements of the pension credit are tax free.

Equity Release

If you own your own freehold property, you could raise capital in order to perhaps buy a new car or caravan or other asset by means of an Equity Release mortgage.

However, doing this simply to gain income (i.e. to buy an annuity) will almost certainly affect any pension credit that you may be entitled to, so by doing so you could be shooting yourself in the foot at the same time as reducing the size of your estate which you may ultimately wish to bequeath.

Perhaps a more sensible form of Equity Release could be to buy a better property than you could otherwise afford. Typically, you could get an equity release mortgage for a third of the value of the property and pay nothing ever - although the mortgage company would receive their funds plus interest on your death, or if / when you go into a nursing home.

For example if you have current equity of £200,000 and want to buy a property for £300,000, you could probably secure an equity release mortgage for the extra £100k at typically 6% interest (compounded).

Assuming you died 20 years later when the house was then worth perhaps £500,000, the capital amount (£100,000) and the interest (approx £220,000) would then be paid, leaving your estate with £180,000.

Obviously, if you have offspring's who are waiting for their inheritances, they may be a bit peeved, or maybe you don't have any. But of course the property might be worth a million in 20 years then your estate would still be worth £680k.

Most UK equity release mortgages are safe in the fact that you would never lose your home while you are living, but you must of course make perfectly sure that it **is** safe and read the small print very carefully and have it all explained by a reliable independent solicitor. Please **do not** take my word for any of this - **check it out thoroughly!**

Do remember that if you use an intermediary agent, their main concern is that they close a deal and therefore secure their fees which you must be fully aware of. And these fees maybe substantial which of course will come off your equity. But there is nothing to stop you going direct to the bank or building society thereby avoiding agents fees.

More information about equity release can found at http://www.keyrs.co.uk/equity-release . I have spoken to Key Finance and they *seem* to be fairly honest and upfront, but I can't over estimate the need for *independent* advice.

Another contact is http://www.agepartnership.co.uk who also give a fairly interesting online calculator, where you can input possible future house price increases and interest rates. But to use their calculator, you need to sign in and leave a phone number. If you don't want bugging leave an incorrect number, as my simple enquiry with these people resulted in a lot of pressure selling, so I can't say that I would recommend them - actually not at all.

Only your mother has got your best interests at heart, and she's probably long gone! **So take extreme care before proceeding.**

Downsize

If you own your own property downsizing could increase your capital income and also lower your outgoings such as utility bills etc.

But of course it's a big step which you should consider very seriously at a time when you are young enough and fit enough to cope with the inevitable upheaval.

But do try and think it through carefully and make sure that you are moving into a suitable property in an area that you are happy with which is close to all the amenities that you want and need.

Having lived in Cyprus, I can tell you that very few ex pats think it through properly when they buy out there. They often buy properties miles from anywhere (when their brains are in holiday mode) with no public transport, then suddenly find themselves trapped and unable to sell.

So think while you still have a full set of marbles:

- Hospitals;
- Doctors / Dentists;
- Shops;
- Transport;
- Crime rate - you can check this at: http://www.police.uk ;
- Stairs or no stairs - they're great exercise, but not too good for falling down;
- Churches, clubs, community activities, other OAPs etc.

Note that if by downsizing you increase your savings, this would inevitably reduce or eliminate any pension credit that you may be eligible for. But of course you may be downsizing to a more expensive property.

Quite likely you would like to stay in your location when downsizing and this is understandable, but note that there is a huge financial North - South divide. As well as properties being substantially cheaper in the North, so is the cost of living - by far. So this is also a point worth considering.

It seems crazy that people earn more in the South East when they are working (due to living costs), but then the basic pension is the same Nationwide. Having lived in the South, East and North I know this to be true.

I loved our time in North Lincolnshire (near Louth) and can tell you that it's a hidden gem. It even rains less there. In fact the weather in Louth is better than down South, and it definitely rains least in the East - but maybe you think that West is best!

Cash back Sites & Loyalty Cards

The two most popular cash back sites are http://www.quidco.com and http://www.topcashback.co.uk . Both of these are worth joining as you really can receive cash back on certain purchases. But they are only worth using as long as you can't get the service or item cheaper elsewhere.

They are particularly worth looking at when:

- Changing any insurance deal;
- Changing car breakdown cover;
- Switching utility providers;
- Changing banks or credit cards;
- Supermarket shopping with a smart phone (to enable certain essential features).

Whichever supermarket you shop at regularly, it's still worth getting all the loyalty cards such as:

- Tesco club card;
- Nectar card (Sainsbury's / Homebase);
- Morrison petrol card;
- Waitrose card;
- Co-op members card;
- Boots Advantage card.

Even if you don't use them very often, bit by bit they add up and they cost you nothing.

Part time Work

Even if claiming pension credit, you could earn up to £10 per week without this effecting your benefit. And no doubt an extra tenner a week could come in handy.

I don't need to list all the possible occupations that you could get involved in as there're absolutely thousands, many of which are seasonal just for a few days - such as being Santa Claus for a few days if you can cope with a load of sticky, screaming sprogs puking all over you; or calling in rowing boats in the summer etc.

In fact there are probably far more temporary part time jobs available than you might imagine. And the young ones are far too greedy to be interested.

Taking a Lodger

Taking a lodger would almost certainly reduce your pension credit, but if your income is above that level anyway this could prove lucrative, although I know that it's not ideal for a most people. I personally would not want anyone else creeping round my home.

But for some, the right type of tenant could give companionship - like Emily Bishop and Norris Cole on Coronation Street - a mutually beneficial love / hate relationship!

This is also tax free up to £4,250 per year (currently).

Increasing Returns on Investments

If you've saved hard for your retirement as we had, the rate of returns from just about all of the High Street banks is a bit of a kick in the nuts, especially when according to the pension credit calculations you are deemed to be receiving 10% on your savings!

My advice is to shop around to get the best *safe* deal and be prepared to change on a regular basis as others become better. But please avoid high risk speculative strategies, or income bonds that promise you a high percentage return, but hidden in the small print you will find that your capital is gradually (or quite quickly) eroding eventually leaving you with nothing. And if you have any cash ISAs, make sure you move them to the highest paying provider, but check that there are no penalties.

A good starting point for financial advice is the Martin Lewis website at: http://www.moneysavingexpert.com .

If you have enough funds and are young enough to cope with the possible grief, then I can thoroughly recommend *buy to let* properties, as this will generally result in a **much** higher yield than any savings investments and at the same time your capital assets (the properties) will increase in value. See my book 'Buy to Let on a Budget' at http://martinwoodward.net .

If you fancy being a bit speculative, gold coins (krugerrands) are not a bad bet - and there's something really comforting about holding a stash of gold coins. But if you do this, make sure you have somewhere safe to keep them. And with regards to pension credit 'investments' you may be able to consider these as personal jewellery which is not counted as an asset, but you would need to look into this!

If all the world's currencies go pear shaped which I wouldn't rule out, then the only things that will be worth anything will be gold, silver, gemstones, land / property, livestock and water. All paper investments including bank accounts and pensions would vanish overnight. Extreme I know, but no one ever expected the last financial crisis!

Annuities

In case you don't know what an annuity is, it's basically an income for life in exchange for capital.

This could be either index linked (rising with inflation) or not. And could be for a single person or a couple with the income adjusted accordingly. The income of course dies with the recipient, so if you snuff it the week after you take it out, they're laughing!

But the rate of annuities today is pathetically poor and in my opinion you're better off holding onto your assets, then at least you retain your choice. It may of course be that they get better in the future - as they certainly can't get much worse.

Ironically until the 2014 budget, anyone who'd saved for their pension in a typical 'pension fund' would have been forced to use a great amount of the pension pot to buy an annuity. Whereas those who'd invested privately would have complete control.

I had this in mind years ago which is why I only have a very small private pension (annuity), the rest I invested in property.

Rent Out Your Garage

If you don't have a car, but do have a garage or parking space, depending on where you live this could be rented out for £10 - £17 per week.

Dig For Victory!

Now I probably don't need to mention this as most OAP's are already doing it. Apart from the savings, of course home grown produce tastes far better than the shop bought equivalent.

And even if you don't have much room, there's a whole host of veggies that can be grown in small spaces like window boxes, balconies or even mushrooms in a cupboard (although I have to say that they can attract flies).

Or look into the possibility of renting an allotment. Sadly they're dying out in many areas due to the value of the land for building etc., although they can be worth looking into. But local community growing projects are very much on the increase in all areas. Why not see if there's one near you? As an example here's the web link for the Sheffield growers: http://growsheffield.com .

If you have the space and inclination, keeping a few hens could further add to your income or at least keep you self sufficient in eggs. However, be ready for complaints if you have a rampant cock, as your neighbours may not appreciate being woken up in the early hours!

But if you can't or don't want to do any of this, buying your produce from such folk will help them as well as giving you better fresh produce at a fair price. It's win, win!

Swap Your Skills

Everybody is good at something and you can bet your life that someone else in your locality is looking for your skills in exchange for something you want.

This could be absolutely anything from babysitting to hedge trimming to teaching / learning music or English etc., the list is endless.

There are several websites dedicated to this, such as http://www.skillbound.com and http://www.localskillswap.com and also a dedicated section for this on http://www.gumtree.com where you can simply *freely* advertise what you have to offer and what you would like in exchange. Everyone's a winner!

Obviously you will need to use some common sense before allowing strangers into your home.

Reducing Your Expenditure

There are many ways to reduce expenditure and if you apply all of them these can amount to substantial worthwhile savings.

These will come in the following categories:

- Budgeting Correctly & Consistently;
- Keep a Contingency Fund;
- Supermarkets & General Shopping;
- Return Faulty Goods;
- Online Shopping;
- Buy Pre Owned;
- Eating Out;
- Downsize to Save on Heating;
- Insulation / Ventilation;
- Solar Panels & Wind Turbines;
- Heating Your Home;
- Make Sure you know What's Watt;
- OAP Discounts;
- The Westfield Scheme;
- Food Banks? - Not for Us Thanks!

And more in their own dedicated chapters:

- Utilities;

- Insurance;
- Motoring;
- Banks, Credit Cards and Loans.

Budget Correctly & Consistently

Keeping accurate records of your income and outgoings consistently is essential if you intend remaining solvent. Most people manage with the day to day expenditure fairly easily, but often neglect the annual expenses. Christmas comes every year without fail and consequently needs budgeting for on a weekly basis to avoid a disaster (or borrowing which is never a good idea). Similarly with holidays, if you budget for them on a weekly basis, you're more likely to actually afford them (or if you can't afford them, at least you'll know about it). And don't forget about repairs and renewals.

I once had a (great) uncle who had a theory on budgeting whereby he would save cash for certain events and put it where it was needed. For instance, cash for servicing his car was kept in the engine compartment and cash for fixing his roof, in the roof! Perhaps this was a bit extreme, but he was a bit of an extreme guy - he was also a tight fisted old git and never left me a bean in his will. He ran off with a 65 year old dolly bird when he was 89 and she got the lot when he finally snuffed it 7 years later!

A less extreme way, is to keep different tins or envelopes for each event. But always save in cash in a secure fireproof place as once it's in your bank account it just sort of vanishes, unless you're clever enough to create compartments in your bank account and stick with them meticulously. This actually can be done with a spreadsheet, or a home budgeting program such as 'Money Manager Ex' (see resources), but you would need to be very strict with yourself and take the trouble to make the correct entries on a regular basis.

So decide now how much you're going spend on who and for what at Christmas / birthdays etc., save on a weekly basis and you will never have a disaster. Christmas is never worth getting into debt for, and if your Xmas shopping needs to be done in Poundland, so be it - we might even rub shoulders!

Keep a Contingency Fund

Included into your budgeting needs to be a contingency fund. I recommend saving 5 - 10% of your income on a regular basis in cash. This amount which of course will increase each week can then be 'borrowed' to take advantage of various half price offers etc. But remember that you must pay it back so that the fund carries on increasing.

Then at the end of the year this fund (which should be substantial) can be used as you see fit. Keeping cash this way gives a feeling of security and it's fun! See: The Richest Man in Babylon *free* in the resources.

Supermarkets & General Shopping

Back in the good old days it was generally accepted that 'pro rata' buying a large box or jar of an item would work out cheaper than two small ones. But now this is not necessarily the case.

In order for the supermarkets to legally 'reduce' an item they must first sell it at a higher price for a certain length of time. So often items are priced artificially high in preparation for the next 'huge reduction' and if you inadvertently buy at the high price, you'd be playing straight into their hands.

So supermarkets are both blessing and a curse. Just about all of them have their good and bad points and they all play the same nasty tricks designed to confuse you into paying higher prices.

For instance off the top of your head which do you think is the best deal for the same item: 397 grams at £2.00 or 340 grams at £1.80? Actually the 397 grams is slightly better. And of course the supermarkets now have a legal obligation to show the price per kilo or 100 grams which would verify this. But often the labels showing this are too small for us oldies to read! And sticking to 'round figures' is simply not confusing enough for us!

Another nasty trick I found recently was a BOGOF on Lloyd Grossman sauces for the 340g jars, but with a stack of *350g* jars on the same shelf, so if you picked a 340g and a 350g by mistake - no BOGOF! This occurs a lot - watch out for it.

Did you know that suppliers pay a premium for eye level shelving? Obviously this is based on the fact that you're more likely to buy what you virtually trip over. In fact these tactics have been going on since the beginning of time. Why do you think God put certain women's assets at eye level (or more or less eye level)? But you invariably find the best stuff on the lower shelves!

And of course we're programmed to think that any product that is more expensive and packaged in a more appealing way is better than something cheaper with no fancy label. This may or may not be true, but more often than not it's the 'middle way'!

Look at bleach for instance. For goodness sake you're going to chuck it down the bog! And even the *best* stuff only kills 99% of 'known nasties' - and let's face it, it's probably the other one that does all the damage!

Having been a driving instructor and instructor trainer for over 30 years I can guarantee to you that the most expensive driving schools were often the worst value, by far!

Make your own genuine comparisons between named brands and supermarket labels. Try a blindfolded taste test and you may be surprised. But forget the washing powders, 'cause they all taste awful!

To be fair to the supermarkets, there are also many genuine half price offers or BOGOFs or money off vouchers (through your door or in papers etc.), obviously designed to get you in there in the hope that you'll spend frivolously on other items. You'd be wise to take advantage of these in a big way - as long as the offers are genuine and for stuff that you really want that is not perishable. Use your contingency money to borrow from yourself to stock up when these occur.

Obviously which supermarkets you use will be dependent on where you live. Where we live there are plenty, so we can compare prices and get the best deals from each.

But all of them will encourage you to buy far more than you need, so be particularly careful not to buy what you might end up wasting. It's estimated that on average families waste £700 per year on food - I see this as a great sin especially when you think how much half of them are in debt, and how much they complain about what they haven't got! No wonder I've got the Victor Meldrew syndrome!

To get the best out of the supermarkets, **don't impulse buy**, write a list and stick to it, with the exception of BOGOFs that you can save and will use. This actually is where men are often better than women. If I have a list I (like most fellas) will stick to it rigidly and just get in and get out with as little grief as possible! Or better still buy on line via http://www.mysupermarket.co.uk .

And don't forget the smaller supermarkets like Farm Foods, Iceland and Jack Fultons, who spend less on advertising. Advertising is expensive and ultimately *you* pay for it!

Finally, if you buy anything where the price has been drastically reduced (near to sell by date etc.) always put these items to the back of the conveyer and double check that they all go through at the correct reduced price. My experience is that *more don't than do!* Then you're simply being ripped off!

Return Faulty Goods

Save all receipts and bills according to how important they are:

- Supermarkets just until you've checked them;
- Clothes for a year;
- Electrical goods until a year after warranty;
- Items with lifetime guarantee forever with packaging;
- Eco light bulbs for the length of the guarantee with a note of where they were used and for how long;

- Utility Bills for a few years to check usage.

And don't be afraid to stand up for your rights when there is a fault. Most supermarkets and places like Argos will refund you without question as long as you have the receipt.

Recently we bought a large jar of pickled onions that were soggy and horrible. As it happens I didn't have the receipt, but as they were the supermarket's own brand they couldn't argue and just refunded me. I know it sounds petty as it was only just over a pound, but it all adds up! And anyway I've got a reputation to keep as being a grumpy old git!

But on a much larger scale, a few years ago we bought a three piece suite for just over £3,000 and the deal was (amazingly); 3 years interest free credit, then after performing a few simple tasks, receive a refund of the total amount. Well if you're like me, you'd think that if it looks too good to be true, it's a con (which it generally is). I read and re-read the small print, cut out and saved the original advert, made the shop manager sign an additional guarantee and bought it.

In order to get the refund, the request had to be made by registered mail at exactly the right time which of course I did. But not surprisingly the offer was underwritten by a third party company who had of course gone bust. But my agreement was with the suite company not the insurance company, so after a few letters and fob offs, I started court action against them. The day before the court case the MD phoned me and offered me half - £1,500 which I accepted as I felt a bit sorry for him - especially as it was good suite which was still good over three years later.

Had it actually gone to court, I probably would have won the full amount as I had all the evidence in writing along with the original newspaper cutting. But the fact that he'd made a good offer might have gone against me and he did plead with me a bit and he was eventually being honourable. Actually, I felt a bit rotten - but as I've said, I have a reputation to keep!

Another thing that seems to happen to us quite a lot is when we go out for a meal, often my wife seems to end up with a duff one. Now, as well as being the world's greatest oracle, my wife is an incredibly good cook, so why the heck should she have to put up with substandard garbage in restaurants? Well she doesn't and she's not afraid to tell them!

The result is that they soon learn, and now jump through hoops for us at all our regular haunts! When we book a table, we don't just get a table, we get the best table, the best service and the best food! Or face the wrath of the wife!

Once I also had a run in with Npower who were convinced that I owed them some money which I knew I didn't. They passed the 'debt' onto a collection agency who started writing me letters and adding £15 on for each letter plus interest.

My response was to write back to Npower with a £15 invoice for each letter that I sent them and an invitation to meet me in court so that I could make them look stupid - as I had absolute proof that they were wrong. After four of my '£15' letters they realised their error and paid me the £60 - which I never actually expected!

The really worrying thing is that so many of the big organisations are 'wrong' on a regular basis and no-one does anything about it!

Online Shopping

Huge savings can be made for just about everything by online investigation. This way you can nearly always find the cheapest price. Then it's down to you whether to buy online; but often your local store will offer a price match which may be the best option, especially if you feel that they may offer a better after care service which is an important factor.

For smallish items such as ink cartridges etc., you'll almost certainly find the best deals on eBay or Amazon.

Any High Street business that wants to survive will also have an online option, if they don't, you will not see them in five years as like it or hate it, it's happening and it's the way forward. Go with the flow!

And always check the cashback sites.

Buy Pre Owned

If you buy a new jacket for say £60 and after wearing it a couple of times decide that you don't like it. How much do you think you'd get for it if you tried selling it? Well I doubt if you'd get half your money back - in fact you probably wouldn't even bother and it would sit there in your wardrobe gathering dust for a couple of years until it doesn't even fit you anymore. Then when you're de-cluttering (good idea) you'd probably end up taking it to the local charity shop - and you've only worn it twice!

The point I'm trying to make is that there must be some pretty good stuff in these places if you can be bothered to look.

Personally, I've never bought anything from a charity shop (but I've given them plenty). In fact I'm not big on buying clothes at all - that's the wife's department. My idea of the perfectly dressed man is / was Mahatma Ghandi. I mean, he only ever wore one item (one size fits all) and that never even needed ironing. And everybody loved him - well, everyone except the bastard who shot him I guess!

But as for buying cars, buying new (unless you own a business and can take advantage of the tax benefits) is basically chucking money down the drain. My tactics are to buy as lower mileage as possible approximately 2 -3 years old for less than half the cost of new.

Over the years I've bought numerous expensive electronic keyboards, mainly second-hand and in many cases have used them for several years and lost nothing on the re-sale. And even the ones that I purchased new, I always negotiated a price far lower than the asking price.

Similarly with furniture, there are some unmarked, *good as new* bargains to be had on eBay, Gumtree, Preloved etc. But you have to know what you are buying!

Eating Out

My wife always likes to eat out on a Saturday night, which to be honest baffles me, but to enter into conflict on this point (or any other point) is just not worth the grief! So we eat out on Saturday nights!

But the best deals are always mid week and / or early evening, obviously because they're less busy times.

If you look on the net, you can more or less always get 2 for 1 deals at places like Ask or Prezzo etc. for the mid week. And if you go mid week or early, you will generally also have better service, better food (as the kitchen is less stressed) and a better environment.

Also there are many good OAP deals to be had. There's a Chinese near us in Sheffield where 'wise ones' can eat as much as they like for £5.50 before 5.00 (Monday to Thursday) - http://www.flaming-dragon.co.uk and the same at Taybarns for £4.49 - http://www.taybarns.com . Both have restaurants in many areas!

I have to say that we don't go to Taybarns very often (despite the fact that it's a really good deal), as I've seen a few warning signs there. Actually I think that there's a few people that they shouldn't let in - I mean, you wouldn't serve someone with alcohol who was clearly drunk would you?

Damon's in Sheffield, Lincoln and Liverpool offer a 25% discount for OAP's and a *free* meal on your birthday! - http://www.damons.co.uk .

And if you live near Sheffield of ever visit, then I can personally recommend the best meal deal that I've ever found at The Old Harrow, Grenoside where you can get **two** *quality* meals for **£5** and they don't even screw you for the drinks as so many do. See:- http://www.oldharrow.co.uk .

There are also many good OAP fish and chip deals just about everywhere so look around.

I've also written to JD Wetherspoons and they are considering my request for OAP discounts, so I am hopeful for this, but they do some pretty good deals anyway.

Why not research the deals in your area and distribute the results to other OAP's?

Downsize to Save on Heating etc.

I mentioned downsizing previously with regards to perhaps increasing income, but of course you could make enormous savings on your bills by doing so, as well as having a property which is easier to clean etc.

And this option is also open to those living in council properties, where you could move to a more manageable property near likeminded individuals and at the same time releasing a valuable larger property for a family who may be in desperate need of it. Surely this is common sense!

Insulation / Ventilation

Now notice here that I've put insulation and ventilation under the same heading - this is because the two are inter-related, yet the latter is often ignored.

Ok, firstly insulation - we're talking *thermal* insulation here. The most common and effective types of insulation are:

- Double or triple glazing;
- Cavity wall insulation;
- Loft insulation (at the correct depth);
- Heavy Curtains;
- Door (and other) draft excluders;
- Under floor insulation and / or suitable carpet underlay.

If you haven't got all of the above, you will be allowing valuable heat to escape and wasting money. If you are claiming pension (guaranteed) credit, you may be eligible for a grant for most of the above as well as an efficient boiler.

Assuming you have done all of the above, you will have the place sealed up like a polythene bag and will be inhaling what you exhaled yesterday - dog farts included - unless the place is also adequately ventilated.

Without ventilation even just by breathing you will create condensation and consequently damp and mould; more so if you cook, or shower, or dry any washing, or use a drier inside.

It is a fact that a dry house is cheaper and easier to heat than a damp house and most dampness is self inflicted. I know this is true and have proved it numerous times.

Now obviously you might think, what's the point of insulating everything if you've then got to ventilate it? Well you can control it, by opening windows *every time* you shower or cook and at night (for the whole night) when you are tucked up warm in bed - especially in the winter - the place will then warm up much more quickly in the morning! Also, leave wardrobe doors open regularly to air them out. Be sure to use jack locks if you live in a bungalow or downstairs flat.

The only alternative to this is if you have a heat exchange unit, but these are really only suitable for self builds being installed at the time of building.

Make no mistake correct ventilation will reduce your fuel bills!

How can you be so sure on this?

I've had several rental properties in the past and all tenants are notoriously bad at opening windows (through ignorance), which ultimately results in serious damage to the property as well as excessive fuel bills. Numerous times I (as a landlord) have been blamed for damp when the tenants have caused it themselves and it infuriates me.

Even the house we live in now had damp and mildew upstairs when we bought it, through the previous owners not opening windows. In *every* case we've cured these problems simply by ventilation. It's so simple even an ant can do it!

In fact Macrotermites that live in Africa and Southeast Asia can only survive at exactly 86 degrees, yet the temperature in their habitats can vary between 35 degrees at night and 104 degrees in the day. And these ingenious little creatures have created colonies with mazelike tunnels and chimney flues that creates a constant temperature and humidity day and night without any power - how clever is that?

A shopping mall called Eastgate in Zimbabwe has been constructed using similar technology keeping a constant temperature day and night.

Finally don't forget that if you use a gas fire (or boiler), or solid fuel heating, you will need the correct ventilation in place to expel dangerous fumes. A carbon monoxide alarm should be fitted to all properties using these types of heating. And subfloor airbricks should always be kept clear to keep your joists aired out.

Radon Gas

Another vitally important reason to make sure that your property is adequately ventilated is to help reduce the effects of radon gas which is one of the greatest links to lung cancer.

You might think that the radon gas problem only affects certain areas (particularly the West), which is true to a point, but basically it comes up from the ground *everywhere* and you can't see it, smell it or hear it.

In most areas simply ventilating your property will eliminate the problem, but if you live in a particularly badly affected area or a basement flat, you would be wise to have it checked out.

See: http://www.ukradon.org for further information.

Solar Panels & Wind Turbines

I personally think that generating your own electricity is the way forward for everyone. But for most the initial cost is prohibitive and will probably remain so.

Firstly, solar panels. There are two types of these and it's very important that you understand the difference, as one of them is basically useless in the UK. And this one is the type that has water circulating through pipes within the panel in order to supposedly generate hot water.

In Cyprus everyone has one of these on the roof along with a hot water tank, and they work great in the summer when it's hot and sunny beyond belief. In the winter they still work on sunny days, although far less efficiently. But in the UK it's simply not sunny enough and hot enough for these to be cost effective or even work at all. At best you'll get warmish water that will require further heating. But of course technology is improving all the time, so who knows in the future?

Now, the other type of solar panels which mustn't be confused with the former are known as photovoltaics (PV). These capture the sun's energy using photovoltaic cells. The cells convert the sunlight into electricity, which can either be stored in a series of batteries or used directly with the remainder being redirected into the national grid for which you would receive a payment (or reduction in your bill).

Again these are also used in Cyprus, but mainly on properties not connected to the grid, so that they can generate and store their own power. The downside is that the batteries and inverter (DC - AC) are very expensive, but still often cheaper than connecting to the grid, but after the initial investment they then have permanent free power that works well.

But here in the UK, you wouldn't need the expensive batteries as what you didn't use would be sold back to the grid and then in the dark when they obviously wouldn't work, you would be using the grid as normal.

Now you might think that the UK is not suitable for these, but it is. They work well even on cloudy days, but they must be fitted to a South facing roof - otherwise they're a waste of time.

Furthermore there are often government subsidies for these, but check as these alter regularly.

So are they worth it for me?

Basically this depends on your circumstances. If you need to borrow to do it, then I would say probably not. But if you have investments that are generating little or no yield and getting rid of some capital could perhaps then enable you to claim pension credit, then I would say that it could be very worthwhile as you could then reduce all future fuel bills dramatically forever!

But it also depends on how long you intend living. Personally I intend living forever and I have to say that *so far* it's going quite well! You have to remain positive about these things!

If you do decide to go ahead, please shop around for the best deal and look at suppliers very carefully and also look into what government grants may be available. But never pay any money upfront (or if you have to make sure it's via a credit card) and don't be taken in by lifetime guarantees, they could be bankrupt tomorrow!

Following is a hypothetical example of how Andy Pandy and Looby Loo made huge savings by installing PV solar panels.

You probably remember this pair, who are now retired. After a 50+ year stormy marriage they now live on a crap pension (from before the days when the BBC started chucking their money about).

After leaving the BBC in 1970 Looby Loo briefly worked as an exotic dancer, but had to give it up because her strings kept getting tangled up. Since then she just stayed at home and looked after the bear - yes they've still got the bear! Andy Pandy worked as a pyjama salesman up until his recent retirement.

Ok, so their sad situation to start with is as follows:

- They have a joint weekly pension income of £180.90;

- Looby Loo has a part time cleaning job (how times change) making an extra £10 per week;

- They own their own (band C) house in Sheffield - they moved North to get a better deal;

- They have savings of £40,000 which means that they are not eligible for the guaranteed element of Pension Credit but they do receive the savings element amounting to £14.94 per week.

So to make it simple their income is shown below:

Andy Pandy & Looby Loo's Income	
Joint Week Pension	£180.90
Looby Loo's Part Time Income	£10.00
Savings Credit	£14.94
Total Income	**£205.84**

Now, I'm going to show you how their income can be increased substantially, simply by reducing their savings a little.

So what they do is:

- Spend £2,500 on a luxury cruise around the Baltic;

- Spend a further £5,000 installing PV Solar panels.

That's it - simple!

But by reducing their £40,000 savings to £32,500 and because of their low income they then become eligible to claim 60p per week of the Guaranteed Pension Credit - no strings attached!

60p a week - Big deal!!!

Yes but that 60p enables them to:

- Claim a 100% refund of their council tax (£1,326.52 per year);

- The savings benefit increases to £20.34 per week. Yes, mad isn't it? Their savings have reduced but the benefit has increased!;

- Free dental work for the few teeth they have left between them;

- Free Chiropodist for Looby Loo's fungal foot infection;

- Free glasses for both of them;

- Increased winter fuel allowance;

- 'Care for the bear' free at the PDSA - he regularly suffers from fur balls and needs re-stuffing about every ten years!;

- Plus other benefits.

In addition to these benefits they also save about £500 per year on their fuel bills due to the solar panels.

So their revised income is itemised below:

Mr & Mrs Pandy's Revised Income	
Joint Week Pension	£180.90
Looby Loo's Part Time Income	£10.00
Savings Credit	£20.34
Guaranteed Pension Credit	£0.60
Council Tax Refund	£25.51
Solar Panel Fuel Savings	£10.00
Total Income	**£247.35**

So, in total their income has increased by £41.51 per week. That's about a 22% increase! And that doesn't include all the additional personal benefits or the free health care for the bear! And they enjoyed the cruise - except the bear who had to stay at home! And of course the savings achieved by the solar panel will increase in real terms as electricity prices continue to increase.

Now if Andy Pandy wasn't such a skinflint, he'd spend another £10,000 of their savings at an antiques jewellery auction and invest in a 5 carat solitaire diamond ring for Looby Loo. Even though this would remain a valuable asset, this would not be counted in the pension credit evaluations, so their income would increase by another £20 per week! Don't we live in a mad world?

To keep the above calculations reasonably simple, I have not included the small amount of interest they would have lost by spending part of their savings, but at current rates this is minimal.

Ok, finally, Wind Turbines. Personally I am great believer in wind power - *as the wife can vouch for*. But to be honest I would say that this is only of use as an additional source of power to the PV panels if you live in a fairly windy and rural area.

The downsides are that they're probably not cost effective and they can also be noisy.

A few years ago B&Q started selling these for about £1,500, but they have since been withdrawn from sale as they didn't work as expected. But who knows in the future? The wind still blows and I'm hopeful that they'll improve these for domestic use in the future.

Heating Your Home

The source of power you use to heat your home can vary tremendously in price, but unfortunately is not always in your control.

The most common of course are:

- Gas;
- Oil;
- Electricity;
- Solid Fuel;
- Or combination of the above.

Oil central heating is probably the most expensive, which is what we used when we lived in Lincolnshire and oil is generally used where gas is unavailable as was the case with us.

If you have to use oil, I would advise against automatically signing up with a supplier, but instead phone round and negotiate with different suppliers. We usually used the same supplier, but nearly always negotiated a cheaper price - simply by asking. Also with oil beware of theft, which unfortunately is beginning to occur in rural areas.

Fortunately while we were in Lincolnshire we also had an open fireplace which we used regularly mainly for free as we lived next to open woodland and I'd just send the wife out in the mornings with an axe to fetch a few trees!

Solid fuel central heating via a back boiler to an open fire or a wood burning or multi fuel stove is probably my favourite form of heating as it can be very efficient and you are less effected by power cuts and strikes etc. The downside is that it can be messy and labour intensive.

Obviously with solid fuel heating there is a fire risk which makes the need for a fire guard and smoke alarm (which you should have anyway) all the more important.

There are also some quite sophisticated semi-automatic solid fuel boilers which work via recycled wooden pellets being fed in according to your instructions.

Electric storage heating can work well with an economy 7 off peak tariff. The downside is that you have to predict tomorrows temperature in advance and if you need to boost the heating without using the off peak rate, you will be paying a fortune.

The modern electric storage heater are far better than older versions.

Using electric fires for heating is prohibitively expensive.

Electric central heating boilers (usually using the economy 10 tariff), so far has not impressed me. One of our sons had this in a flat and his bills were astronomical. But they may improve in the future.

Another type of electric heating is the electric under floor heating. This works well in a small spaces where a radiator may get in the way (perhaps a kitchen) and is easy and economical to fit, but watch running costs.

The good thing about electric heating (without the boiler) is that there will be no boiler to service or breakdown, so this must be a consideration.

If you generate your own electricity via solar panels etc., then of course electric heating may be a good option for you.

But by far the most common type of heating is gas central heating and / or gas fires mainly because it's:

- easy to control;
- clean;
- efficient; and
- it's the cheaper than oil or electricity (at the moment).

Whichever fuel source you use, a modern efficient condensing boiler with radiator valves in each room will no doubt be more cost effective *to run*. If you have an old inefficient boiler and are on pension credit, you may be eligible for a grant for a new boiler.

However, if you are not on pension credit, if your old boiler is working fine, I would think carefully before changing it as although the new condensing boilers are more efficient heat wise, my experience with them is that they are more expensive to buy and are not as reliable as the older type - so ultimately may not be quite as cost effective as you may imagine.

With all forms of wet central heating, periodically your radiators should have a power flush to increase their efficiency. Always shop around for this as the price can vary considerably for the same job.

Beware of monthly maintenance schemes such as the British Gas 'Homecare' scheme. Read the small print carefully so that you are fully aware of exactly what is and more importantly *isn't* covered - you may be surprised!

I'm not saying that you shouldn't have a maintenance contract, - although I personally think that they are a waste of money - just that you should shop around!

Make Sure You Know What's Watt!

Now in the world of electricity there's an awful lot of watts, and these mustn't be confused with James Watt, who was the Watt what invented steam engines. Here we're talking about watts what float about in electric wires. Cunning little blighters they are as you can't even see them, but if you don't understand them it's them what costs you a fortune!

So, in order to minimise electric costs, you need to know what's watt especially as electric costs are spiralling out of control.

In case you don't know, a kilo watt is a thousand watts and uses 10 times more than a 100 watt light bulb. And of course although the lighting is comparatively low wattage it will also be used more continually, so changing to low wattage LED lighting where a typical 60w incandescent (traditional) bulb replaced by a 8w LED will significantly reduce your bills.

Typically the most expensive appliances to run use 3 kilo watts and would be anything that generates heat.

I've listed just a few of the most common appliances below.

High Usage Appliances
Electric Cooker / hob • Electric Fire • Immersion Heater

Electric Kettle • Storage Heater • Hair Drier

Iron • Toaster

Medium Usage Appliances
Vacuum Cleaner • Fridge /Freezer • 100w lighting

500w security lighting • Blender / Mixer

Low Usage Appliances
TV Digi Box • Computer / Laptop • Router

Flat Screen TV / Video • Eco Low Wattage Lighting

And just when you've finally discovered what's watt, guess what? You've then got to learn your bloomin' 'lumens'. They're not satisfied with just changing old pounds to new pounds, pounds and ounces to kilograms, pints and gallons to litres, feet and inches to metres, now they want to confuse us even more!

You may or may not know that there are two different types of new energy efficient light bulbs which are slowly replacing the existing incandescent bulbs that we are all used to. These are LED's (light emitting diodes) and CFL's (compact fluorescents). Both are more expensive to buy than the incandescent bulbs, but both last much longer, are far more energy efficient and will ultimately help reduce your electric bills considerably. If you want to use a dimmer switch, you must buy a special bulb or a compatible dimmer switch (in both cases).

Now the lumen is a measurement of 'light output' and to give you an idea how many lumens you may need, the following chart will give you some comparables.

Light Output	LED	Incandescent	CFL
Lumens	Watts	Watts	Watts
450	4 - 5	40	9 - 13
800	6 - 8	60	13-15
1,100	9 - 13	75	18-25
1,600	16 - 20	100	23-30
2,600	25 - 28	150	30-55

The chart also shows that LED lighting uses less than 20% electricity than it's incandescent equivalent. They also last about 20 years (allegedly).

Many people (us included) were put off buying these new bulbs due to the quality of light - but they have improved enormously and the technology is improving all the time. And some even produce a similar soft light to the incandescent.

A really good place to see these in action and get them at a decent price is to go to Ikea, that is if you've got a day to spare to get round it and you can cope with the exercise.

OAP Discounts

There are many organisations offering various discounts to OAP's both nationally and no doubt locally.

Here's just a few of the national ones:

- B&Q 10% on Wednesdays, this can be substantial if planning any major projects (but kitchens and bathrooms are excluded);
- Cinemas;
- Rail Cards;
- National Express.

Links for the above and more are shown in the resources section. But do look into the local ones as well as there are many - always ask if there's a OAP discount, even if it's not advertised.

The Westfield Health Scheme

If you are *not* claiming pension credit and you still have a few teeth, wear glasses and got dodgy feet, the Westfield Health Scheme is guaranteed to be worthwhile for you. Even at the basic level of £5.65 per month you would be entitled to claim back:

- Up to £31 per year for dental;
- Up to £35 per year for chiropody;
- Up to £45 every other year for optical;
- Plus many other benefits.

In fact, it's not really worth not doing - I just can't see how they stay in business, but they've been around for quite a few years.

See: http://www.westfieldhealth.com or call 0114 250 2000 for more details.

Food Banks? - Not for Us Thanks!

The welfare system in the UK is certainly one of the most generous in the world, (which is no doubt why half of the rest of the world are trying to get here), and yet food banks have begun to emerge at an alarming rate.

Now don't misunderstand me, if anyone genuinely needs these, they are a blessing without a doubt, but to take advantage of them when receiving adequate benefits is clearly wrong.

If any pensioner thinks they need food banks, first they should check that they are receiving their correct entitlements and (if necessary) deal with any debt issues. And even single parents receive more than adequate benefits for their *needs,* although they may well get their *needs* mixed up with their *wants!*

I've no doubt that some people will find these words offensive. But I can assure you that they're not spoken by some 'toff' who knows nothing about scrimping and scraping to make ends meet.

In the winter of 77/78 when I was working as a self employed driving instructor in a depressed area, we had particularly bad snow and ice which lasted for three months continuously. This coupled with the 'gritter strike' prevented me from earning *anything* during this period, and being self employed, I wasn't entitled to any benefits - despite the kids. Then when the snow stopped, the drive shaft on my car bust putting me off the road for a further three weeks waiting for the part - then it snowed again, but fortunately not for very long.

To survive we used the credit card. And I borrowed from the bank to pay the credit card, then borrowed from the credit card to pay the bank - not something that I would particularly recommend, but we had no choice - we were desperate. Basically it took us a full year of hardship to recover financially from this period.

So I know only too well what it's like to eat nothing but potatoes for over six months. But we survived - and it didn't do the kids any harm either - I don't think so anyway. There's a picture of one of them below.

He's definitely got his mother's ears bless him!

And her moustache!

But clearly many 'hardships' are self induced, caused by drugs, alcohol, gambling, debt and general mismanagement of personal affairs. And however much money is pumped into the welfare system, it will never be enough to gratify the '*needs*' of many.

It's actually the single *genuine* jobseekers (with no kids to use as cash cows) who I feel for most, as even Einstein couldn't make their benefits match their outgoings if they live alone and have household utility bills to pay - they simply don't compute. So clearly they and others who may have slipped through the net *need* the food banks - but we don't!

Insurance

A certain amount of insurance in order to protect yourself against loss is wise, as long as it's bought at the right price, gives the correct level of cover and is genuinely needed.

In all cases, when taking out insurances always read the small print thoroughly as they are nearly all riddled with ambiguities, and remember that different companies offer different levels of cover.

Another point to consider with all insurances is that many use premium rate phone numbers (0844 / 0870 etc.) and also *administration fees* as a way of creating extra 'hidden' charges. Make sure that you are aware of all these.

Below are the insurances that you are most likely to need:

- Life Insurance;
- Buildings & Contents;
- Drains / water leakage;
- Holiday Insurance;
- Boiler Maintenance;
- Home Appliance;
- Motor Vehicle;
- Breakdown;
- Extended Vehicle Warranty;
- Pet Insurance.

Life Insurance

Quite likely you have some form of life insurance in place, probably one that will simply pay out a sum to help with funeral expenses. To change to a different company after one of these has been running for a while is probably not cost effective, but it is always worth checking to see that what you have is fair.

If you feel that you will have enough funds left in your estate to cater for your final journey then you may consider this an unnecessary expense and an unnecessary drain on your limited funds.

Buildings & Contents

If you own your own house, not having buildings and contents insurance would be irresponsible.

But levels of cover and prices vary enormously. To start with decide what you actually need i.e. 'buildings catastrophe insurance' and contents 'fire, theft and flood' - then start adding on all the extras from there. If you want insurance for accidental breakage and jewellery etc., then you will have to pay accordingly.

In all cases there will be a minimum excess which you will have to pay in the event of a claim. And of course if you do make a claim, your next yearly premium will increase accordingly.

My personal tactic is to have the very lowest priced basic cover for buildings and contents.

If you live in a rented property of course you will only need contents cover.

Drains / Water Leakage

If you have a water meter and then have a leak or burst your side of the meter, you will be liable for the cost of the water loss as well as the repair.

The water companies are always happy to remind you of this and will offer you over priced cover for this eventuality.

Actually the chances of a leak are very low and you need to decide whether it's worth taking the risk. Also this cover and drain cover maybe included in your buildings insurance.

If you live in a rented property this is not applicable.

Holiday Insurance

If you intend venturing abroad on holiday, you would be totally mad not to take out holiday insurance even if you have the NHS E111 card (which you should get anyway). The E111 card will give you basic reciprocal health care in EU countries at the general hospitals (who probably don't speak English) but will not repatriate you.

Having private holiday insurance will enable you to go to the better private clinics (who probably will speak English) and benefit from free repatriation if necessary.

We've found http://www.staysure.co.uk to be ok and they don't charge extra for a whole host of pre-existing conditions which it's absolutely essential that you should declare. If you become seriously ill in a foreign country and find that you don't have the correct cover (or have not declared any pre existing conditions) the results could be devastating. Only a complete moron would attempt travelling without adequate cover.

If, because of pre-existing conditions insurance is too expensive or unavailable to you, then you may want to consider the delights of the UK. I've travelled abroad extensively over the years, I've even experienced the delight of watching water go down the plughole clockwise in the Southern Hemisphere, but rarely have I found better scenery than we have in Wales, Scotland and the Lake district. And there are secluded beaches that you wouldn't imagine in the Scottish Western Isles. And prehistoric sites on Orkney - plus all our castles, stately homes, national parks, rivers / canals and churches - we live in a gem!

Ironically British citizens born before September 2nd 1929 can apply for a free passport. They probably wouldn't get travel insurance but at least they can have free passport!!!

Boiler Maintenance Insurance

Central heating boiler insurance is a difficult one. There are many covers available, British Gas 'Homecare' to name one. Often these are taken out thinking that cover is for all eventualities, but it isn't. Read the small print and then decide whether or not it's worth it for you.

Personally I don't think it is worth it, but you must make up your own mind about this.

Home Appliance Insurance

If you insured all of your white goods and electrical appliances against breakdown you would probably find the cost prohibitive. You probably have the following at the very least:

- TV / Digi Box;
- Washing Machine / Drier;
- Fridge / Freezer;
- Oven / Hob / Extractor;
- Vacuum Cleaner;
- Stereo;
- Computer / Printer.

Let's face it, they all have a limited life. My opinion is that if they last 3 years, anything beyond that is a bonus, so we never bother with this type of cover with the possible exception of a really expensive fridge freezer.

Also guard against extended warranties when you buy an item (unless they are included in the price) as the 1979 Sale of Goods Act states that an item should be 'fit for purpose'. And if it fails within a reasonable time (even outside of the warranty period) you may have a right to claim - although it's a big grey area!

Motor Insurance

If you are fortunate enough to be able to afford a car, you will know that motor insurance is compulsory. If you are one of the many who simply pay what is asked of you from your existing insurers on renewal, you are almost certainly being ripped off, possibly by an awful lot.

I always make extensive checks each year and it always pays off.

Your premium cost will be determined by:

- Your vehicle;
- Your Postcode;
- Your Age;
- Your Driving record (accidents / claims / endorsements etc.);
- Other drivers on the policy.

So it's impossible to give any meaningful comparables. But whatever your circumstances, you can bet that there will be a wide variation in the prices offered to you for essentially the same cover.

But as always they are trying to confuse us. In years gone by there were three types of cover:

- Third Party;
- Third Party Fire and Theft;
- Fully comprehensive.

Ok, these still exist except that the comprehensive cover now is very varied, some including:

- No claims protection;
- Breakdown cover;
- Windscreen insurance;
- Availability of hire car in various events;
- Continental cover;
- Legal assistance etc.;
- And of course all have varying excess premiums.

Another strange thing about car insurance is that it's often cheaper if you put on an extra driver (as long as they don't have a bad record).

As a vague comparison my last year's comprehensive cover was £175, but curiously it was £225 the previous year.

If you think that you had a decent price last year and simply renew your policy with the same company, you will almost certainly be paying too much. Check the comparison web sites before each renewal to find the best price and then complete the deal through 'quidco' or 'topcashback' to also get cash back!

Breakdown Cover

I bet you can remember the good old days when motorists would stop to help one another in trouble.

In 1973 my exhaust pipe lost a bracket and hit the deck when I was on my way home from a night club at 3:00 am. A passing police patrol man stopped and fixed it for me - yes he grovelled underneath for a complete stranger! Can you imagine such a thing happening today? You're more likely to get booked for faulty emissions. So these days, if you intend travelling outside of your locality some form of breakdown cover is advised.

What level of breakdown cover you may require (if any) will be dependent on how far you intend driving. If you just want to potter around very locally, you may decide not to have any at all. But if you intend going on a motorway even once, you would be mad not to be covered as the cost of being towed off a motorway can run into hundreds of pounds.

The main companies offering roadside assistance and repatriation are:

- The AA;
- The RAC;
- Green Flag;
- Tesco, Co-op etc. usually with AXA;

- AutoAid Breakdown
  http://www.autoaidbreakdown.co.uk .

To be honest there's not an awful lot of difference between the different companies and none of them wave at you anymore!

All offer a choice of:

- Basic roadside assistance;

- Relay (repatriation nationwide);

- Relay plus home start;

- Continental cover.

And all offer cover for the car or the driver (in any vehicle). But from time to time there is a fair price variation and some limit the amount of callouts - so always check the small print!

Over the years I've been with all of them but right now I'm with the Green Flag because they offered the best price. But next time it could be any of them. Very often there are offers where you may get a M&S voucher etc.

Research the best then deal that suits your needs and then buy via 'quidco' or 'topcashback' to get cash back!

Extended Vehicle Warranty

When you buy a new vehicle, you quite rightly get a warranty lasting at least one year, although now more often three years or even five. In all cases there will be stipulations insisting that the vehicle must be correctly serviced at the required intervals using the correct original parts.

But once the manufacturer's warranty has expired, you are effectively 'on your own' and will have to pay for any malfunctions which could be substantial in the case of an engine or gearbox failure. An extended warranty can give you some peace of mind to cover these unlikely events. But very often the cost of these can be prohibitive and the cover not very comprehensive - read the small print. And in all cases there will be strict service requirements.

Basically it's a gamble and you need to weigh up the risk against the premium. Personally I don't think they're worth it.

Pet Insurance

If you have a pet, you will no doubt be aware of the cost of vet charges. Pet cover as with everything else comes with a variety of options to choose from.

In most cases there will be an excess to pay and usually dental problems will be excluded. We've recently had to pay £200 to have our cat's teeth sorted out.

And unless you pay a higher premium to start with, as your pet gets older (or if you change companies) the price invariably goes up.

If you are on pension credit, you can get free pet care from the PDSA. http://www.pdsa.org.uk .

Utilities

We come from an era when loyalty was rewarded. But sadly those days are long gone.

Whether it be utilities, banks, insurance or whatever, you will invariably be offered a fairly good deal to start with which **always** gets worse after a while.

Clearly the companies are banking on you being too lazy or to loyal to do anything about it, which is why you must be continually astute and unfortunately will need to change companies (or at least threaten to) on a regular basis. And doing so *will* save you **hundreds of pounds** a year.

Can you afford not to take this advice?

Gas / Electric

It's a sad fact that most of our power suppliers are owned by foreign money making conglomerates who's only motive is profit. And furthermore it's likely that your joint gas / electric bill will increase each year at a much higher percentage rate than your state pension increase, in many cases wiping away all of your increase.

So what can I do about this?

Only what we've talked about earlier - insulation, ventilation, low wattage eco bulbs and if you can sensibly afford it; self sufficiency (via PV panels). And of course shop around for the best deal.

I don't need to tell you to turn off unnecessary lights or don't heat rooms that you're not using - you've been telling your kids that for years.

Finally if you're sitting in your house sweating in a tee shirt in the winter, you might have your heating turned up a notch too high!

Right now we are with First Utility, who seem as reasonable as they get. We've also used OVO who were also ok. But who will be cheapest for you really depends on your individual circumstances.

Comparison Websites

There are many comparison websites listed in the resources, but remember their main concern is to get you to change suppliers (so that they get their whack) so make sure that you input the correct information into their calculations otherwise you will get an incorrect result. In order to supply the correct information you will need to keep your bills for at least a year.

When you've found the best deal, before switching, look into doing the deal via 'quidco' or 'topcashback' to get cash back!

Water

All new homes now are required to be fitted with a water meter, but if you don't have one fitted the chances are that you (as a couple) will be much better off with one and certainly so as a single person. Unlike other utilities, you won't have a choice of suppliers, you're simply stuck with the one who supplies your area even though they're privatised profit driven companies.

Meter deals vary from area to area. Some have a single meter rate, while others have two tariff options; one with a charge per amount used and no standing charge, the other with a monthly standing charge and a lower usage charge. If you perhaps go away for a few months a year, then the 'no standing charge' option would obviously be best for you. Otherwise you would need to monitor your usage and decide which is the best deal for you. If you are unable to do this yourself, the water company *should* help you get the best deal.

Having decided to have a meter fitted, all of a sudden you will become far more aware of water wastage. Ways of saving water are:

- Buy a water butt to save water from your guttering to water the garden;

- Don't use a hosepipe to wash the car (if you have one);

- Shower rather than bath using a water saving device fitted to the shower, and turn the shower off when getting soaped up;

- Use an eco washing machine;

- Use a dual flush toilet if possible, if not you can adjust the cistern to use less water or add a bag of stones;

- Flush the toilet less. Now I'm not suggesting that you should flush the loo after each scream but not after each whisper, or even if you should leave it three months until it gets really bad. All I'm saying is that it costs you about 4p every time you flush it. You make up your own mind!

Telephone (Landline)

The chances are that you will want or need a landline telephone, particularly if you want to combine this with an internet connection which is what most people do (me included). But it's not necessarily essential as you'll see shortly and you will need to work out a balance between economy and convenience to suit your individual usage.

The most common suppliers are:

- BT British Telecom;

- Plusnet;

- Post Office;

- Talk Talk;
- Sky;
- Virgin Media;
- Primus.

You'll find that they'll all offer various packages which may or may not include the line rental (which of course you must have). And very often they have 'offers' where the first period of time is at a lower rate. You must naturally take this into account to calculate an average fee for the total contract time which may be 12 months or 18 months (or whatever).

Right now we use Plusnet with broadband internet included and anytime UK telephone calls which suits us. With all the providers you can also choose to have free calls or perhaps just evening and weekends if this suits you better.

Note that different providers consider evenings and weekends to start / finish at different times - some start at 6:00pm, others at 7:00pm. And note that the 'free' calls will generally last for 60 minutes only and you will be charged (big time) if you exceed this, unless you end the call and redial - so always check the time!

In the past we have used the Post Office (who were fine), Talk Talk who were a complete nightmare and BT who we left because they used call centres in India and I just couldn't understand what they were saying - please note this is *not* a racist comment, just a fact!

Telephone Preference Service

Whichever service provider you decide to go with you'll find that there are more and more people trying to either sell you something you don't want or con you over the phone. Personally I think that any cold callers are an infringement on my privacy which is why I have registered with the **Telephone Preference Service** which makes cold calling illegal.

Registering for this service is free and simple and can be done online at http://www.callpreventionregistry.co.uk or by calling

0800 652 7780. This will filter out most of the unwanted garbage, but we are still getting fairly regular calls from con merchants who are suggesting that there's a fault on my computer. This is a well known trick where they can actually damage your computer if you follow their instructions and go along with them, then they'll ask you for £100+ to fix the problem - and if you pay them that's just the beginning! We just tell them that we haven't got a computer and they go away for a while. Obviously this is probably from outside of the UK as their phone numbers are always hidden (unsurprisingly).

Mobile Telephone

Quite likely you have a mobile telephone in which case you should obviously understand them, but there are many of us oldies who've never had one and don't want one. To be honest I hardly ever use mine - but actually you probably need one.

Why?

The main reason you might need one, is just for the odd emergency, mainly because the old telephone boxes are gradually dying out. If your car breaks down or you have an accident you will find one very useful and that's virtually all I use mine for.

Now if you've never owned a mobile before, choosing the right one for your needs can be mind boggling to say the least.

Basically there are two types of mobiles:

- The basic ones that simply make phone calls and maybe take photos; and

- Smart phones which connect to the internet and can be used for a whole range of applications from watching videos, surfing the web, reading books, listening to music, playing games, sending emails etc., as well as taking photos and making phone calls.

The 'smart phones' are the ones you'll see glued to all the youngsters who have to have therapy if they parted from them for more than about two minutes.

Very often the smart phones can be very expensive to buy and also expensive to run if there is a monthly contract involved.

All phones can be operated on a 'pay as you go' basis which is what I use. But if you connect up to the internet and are not *signed into* a free wifi zone your credit will erode in minutes and this can happen even accidentally if you don't turn off the *data roaming*.

Even the pay as you go packages can be expensive if you get the wrong deal.

I'm guessing that you are more likely to need the basic type of phone on the cheapest network, but even this can be a bit complicated.

When you buy a basic phone it will be either 'locked' to a network like Orange, Virgin or Vodafone etc., where you would have to use their network and call charges, or it will be 'unlocked' and you would then be free to use whichever provider you choose.

I'm on a PAYG with http://www.lycamobile.co.uk and their call charges (at the time of writing) are 5p a minute to call a UK landline, 29p per minute to call a UK mobile and free to all other lyca users. However if you happen to want to call China it's only 1p a minute - personally I think that's right bargain, I just wish I could understand what they're saying!

Now I'm not saying that lycamobile is the cheapest, but it's certainly one of the cheapest and as my usage is so low (about £5) a year, it just doesn't bother me.

As with just about everything like this prices will vary according to your needs and usage, but in all cases you will need a compatible SIM card (as shown below) from the relevant provider (lyca, vodafone etc.). These cost from free to about £5.

The SIM card is inserted in the phone as per the relevant instructions and then as long as you have credit on the card and are in a suitable reception area, your phone will work.

If travelling abroad with your mobile phone, the charges will go through the roof and you will be charged even for receiving calls. If you are going for a long time, you'll find it cheaper to buy a local PAYG SIM card or use Toggle (see resources).

The phone number is attached to the SIM card, so if you change SIMs, then the number will change as well unless you ask for a PAC migration code from your old provider, then the number can be transferred to your new provider. It's often easier to get used to the new number!

If you use your mobile very infrequently like me, you must not forget to charge it up. I leave mine switched off virtually all the time (to preserve the charge) and then just switch it on when I happen to need it - as I use it entirely for emergency outgoing calls.

Most basic mobiles will allow you to store frequently used numbers. I would advise that you store the following numbers in there:

- All your bank and credit card phone numbers;
- Motor breakdown number;
- Motor insurance;
- Home insurance;
- Next of kin.

Hopefully you can see the sense in all the above, especially if your credit / debit cards get lost or stolen, you'll need the phone number from the stolen card urgently! Or if you are involved in an accident and unconscious, this will enable the police to contact your relatives etc.

One final very important point about mobiles is that if you have very low outgoing phone usage, you may be able to dispense with the need for a landline. But then you would also need a mobile internet connection as well, but this could still work out cheaper for you.

Do also be aware of the fact that anyone phoning you (on your mobile) will be paying a high rate, unless they are perhaps on the same network as you. In this event having a PAYG phone with a *dual* SIM may be a good idea.

The new Nokia X android smart phone, shortly to be available in the UK has an unlocked dual SIM and is sensibly priced.

Say No to 0870

Now you probably know that all 0800, 0808 and 0500 numbers are free from landlines (not mobiles). And you should also know that numbers start '07' are to mobiles and could cost you a lot more and will not be included in 'anytime' call packages.

No doubt you are aware that numbers starting '09' could cost you an absolute packet. These are generally used by astrological reading lines or to spend a few minutes talking dirty to 'Luscious Lucy' etc. If you are not an idiot or a pervert, you will no doubt avoid these numbers at all costs.

But in my opinion the worst of the worst are the 0844, 0845 & 0870 numbers which are often used by insurance companies, banks and even the some of the government lines. These won't cost anything like the '09' numbers, but there will nearly always be a connection charge and a 'per minute' charge depending on your service provider.

Personally I simply refuse to call these numbers, but there is a way round it by going to http://www.saynoto0870.com where you can input the number and usually find an alternative which will cost you the standard rate (or free if you have the 'anytime' call package). This is a free service which has never failed me.

Internet Connection (via Landline)

All of the telephone call providers also provide an internet service as an add on to the telephone service. Similar to the telephone service, there's always lots of options to confuse you, particularly with 'usage'.

If you're fairly new to the internet, your usage will be quite low and the lowest usage package will most likely suffice. What takes up most usage is downloading films or TV.

My usage allowance with Plusnet is 10 gigabytes per month which is the lowest / cheapest package and this works for me *just*. But I do quite a lot of uploading large music files to my websites.

Mobile internet

Now should you decide not to have a landline telephone, you would still be able to connect up to the internet (should you wish) by using a mobile service.

These work using the same network as mobile telephones and need a SIM card from your chosen network provider inserted into a 'dongle' which is attached to your PC via a USB socket. As with phones, the dongle may be locked to a particular network or unlocked and therefore suitable for any.

Below is a typical dongle attached to a USB socket. There is also a slightly larger wifi version (that doesn't need plugging in).

Mobile internet is also very useful if you are travelling which is when I use it. I've just had my dongle unlocked (Heaven forbid) and now use low cost Giffgaff - or free Fon when possible.

The most common providers for mobile internet are:

- Vodaphone;
- Three.co.uk;
- Orange;
- Giffgaff;
- Toggle (ideal for UK & Europe).

The downside to using mobile internet is that the cost per gigabyte of usage is quite high - *except for the free Samba*. But if you only have low usage and are saving the cost of a landline contract, it may prove beneficial to you.

Most of the above providers offer a PAYG (pay as you go) service as well as monthly contracts.

Free Wifi

You may have noticed that many establishments (such as McDonalds, Asda and many hotels / cafes) now offer free wifi. This is mainly designed for the mobile smart phones which all the youngster have, but also works for laptops and tablets. The main problem that you may have (certainly with McDonalds) is that the first time you connect they will ask for your mobile number in order to text you a code. So if you don't have a mobile phone or you don't have it with you, you'll be snookered.

Another way of obtaining free internet is at many public libraries. In most cases you can use their computers and internet connection freely. And in some cases you can take your own laptop and just use their internet connection for free. This is a great service, but how long it will last for I don't know.

If you add a *Fon* router to your existing landline system, you will be able to access free mobile internet connections at millions of hotspots throughout Europe. See https://corp.fon.com/en .

Skype

Skype which is owned by Microsoft is particularly useful for contacting friends and family who may live abroad. As against telephone calls Skype is completely free from one Skype user to another and enables audio and video as well as instant messaging.

To use Skype you will ideally need a webcam which most laptops have built in and then simply sign up to the free service at http://www.skype.com/en and you're off. Skype can also be operated from smart phones.

In addition to the free service you can also make low cost calls to landline and mobile numbers anywhere in the world from your computer. I've found this particularly useful when travelling across the EU, but you would of course need an internet connection, which are available either free or for a small charge at most EU campsites and Hotels etc.

Due to the video, Skype uses are fair amount of memory. A typical one hour connection (with video) uses 250 - 350 MB.

Sky TV

I suppose if you happen to be a huge sports fan or want to see all the latest films before they hit the free channels then paying for the various Sky TV packages maybe worthwhile to you.

For me it's certainly a monthly expense that I can do without, but of course everyone is different.

Everything that I want to watch is on 'freeview' or 'freesat', which gives me hundreds of channels to watch and with a *hard drive* freeview box, up to two channels at a time can be also recorded. And one of the really good things about losing your memory is that you will have forgotten that you've seen all the repeats! I keep watching all the Poirot episodes over and over and sometimes get the vague feeling that I've seen them before, but I never remember who did it!

If you live in an area where reception for terrestrial is not good, then fitting a dish pointing to Astra 2 (which is approximately 145 degrees SE depending on your location) and using 'freesat' could be your best option.

Or as mentioned earlier, if you have an unlimited broadband connection an XBMC smart box will enable you to receive 'catch up TV' such as:

- BBC iPlayer;
- ITV Player;
- 4 on Demand;
- Demand 5etc;
- Plus many free sports and film channels.

So basically, you can watch anything you like whenever you like and get rid of all the adverts.

To recap:

- Terrestrial TV comes via an aerial (freeview);
- Satellite TV comes via a dish (freesat);
- Smart TV comes via a broadband connection but needs a smart TV or XBMC smart box.

All of the above are free to view, so why pay for Sky?

Unfortunately, all require a TV licence until you reach the tender age of 75 when it finally becomes free.

Motoring Costs

Ok, you've probably had a car for many years and you probably think you know how much it's costing you. And up until retirement, you've managed the cost without thinking about it too much.

But having reached retirement, you'll almost certainly find that running a car is one of your most costly outgoings, which is fine as long as you are fully aware of these costs and you can genuinely afford them.

The Real Cost of Motoring

So let's just have a brief look at exactly what the cost of motoring entails:

- Purchase cost of vehicle;
- Finance charges for purchase (if applicable);
- Fuel;
- Road tax (varies according to emissions);
- Insurance (which will increase as you get older);
- Breakdown cover (AA / RAC etc.);
- General maintenance (tyres, servicing, repairs etc.);
- Parking fees;
- Unexpected major repairs;
- Annual MOT;

- Depreciation of vehicle.

If you realistically add all this lot up, it might be more than your disposable income (after essentials) in which case you simply can't afford to run a car!

When I passed my driving test in 1966 my grandfather gave me the following advice: "For every penny that you spend on petrol - put the same amount away for running costs and repairs."

Over the years I've followed this advice and it works pretty much bang on. **BUT** this assumes you have accrued a full 65% no claims insurance record and it also doesn't take into account depreciation which will usually be the same amount again.

So to be realistic you can reckon that if you spend £20 per week on fuel it will cost you another £20 per week for running costs and *another* £20 per week for depreciation. Frightening isn't it? But if you think that you can do it cheaper, you're probably kidding yourself. Unless you're one of the very rare breeds who can buy a second-hand car, run it for a year, then sell it for a profit, which I know *is* possible, but in 48 years of motoring I've never managed it!

And even if you cut right down on your mileage, (which is certainly a good idea), you will save on fuel, but pro rata the other costs will go up (as many are constant).

The Banger Alternative

Surely there must be a cheaper alternative?

Well my next door neighbour Mike proved to me that there is, although it's not what I'd call *100% reliable*, but it saves him a fortune! He's not a fool - he knows that paying off his mortgage early is far more sensible than having a flash car!

His tactic is to buy a banger with a full years MOT (or near enough) for about £500 - £600 and then simply run it into the ground after which the vehicle is scrapped for about £150. So with this method if you're lucky, you may get a full years (or more) motoring for £350 (£500 purchase less the £150 scrapping price).

Obviously with this tactic, you don't waste money on servicing apart from the most basic of safety checks (brakes, tyres, bulbs etc.), but remember you would always start with a full MOT guaranteeing initial safety.

Another really good thing about this option is that you never have to get upset about the *supermarket trolley knocks* which can cause a coronary on a new car! My advice on this one incidentally is to park well away from the supermarket main entrances which is where just about everyone else *wants* to park.

See: http://www.bangernomics.com .

Keeping Motoring Costs Down

As always knowledge is power, so make sure you know the full running costs of your vehicle per mile. It's crazy that when buying a car we're quoted miles per gallon (mpg), yet we are sold fuel by the litre, so in order to calculate your correct cost per mile you really need to know the miles per litre (mpl).

To make this simple for you I've created a very easy calculator which will enable you work out the true cost per mile. Go to: http://martinwoodward.net/pen2.html to download this free.

To calculate an accurate mpg:

- First fill up with fuel to the very top;
- Set the trip meter to zero, use at least half the tank;
- Fill up again (to the top) and note the mileage;
- Add the fuel cost and mileage covered to my calculator which will then automatically show your correct mpg.

Then working out an accurate cost per mile or per journey is easy, by simply adding the mpg (and fuel cost) to the calculator.

The default figures in the calculator show the running costs of my 1.9 Seat Altea turbo diesel which equates to about 14p per mile for fuel and the same again for running costs. Or about £2,200 for 8,000 miles (a typical year for me), but this *excludes* depreciation. And of course I have researched the very cheapest insurance deal and breakdown cover.

Note that your mpg can be improved considerably by:

- Not using your vehicle for very short journeys;
- Keeping your speed down - exceeding 60mph will reduce (worsen) your mpg significantly;
- Avoiding accelerating to red lights;
- Avoiding harsh acceleration or braking;
- Driving smoothly and gently at all times;
- Maintaining correct tyre pressures;
- Servicing your vehicle within the manufacturers guidelines;
- Changing to a more economical vehicle.

Further savings can be made by making sure that you buy your fuel at the cheapest local price.

So what about the difference between fuels?

Well obviously you should use the correct fuel for your vehicle.

Basically there are four engine / fuel options:

- Petrol;
- Diesel;
- LPG conversion;
- Electric, or part electric (hybrid).

Petrol engines are cheapest to buy, but use the most fuel according to the engine size. But a small, light vehicle with a petrol engine is probably the most economic option when purchase costs and depreciation are added to the equation.

Diesel engines use less fuel than petrol engines although diesel is slightly more expensive. Diesel engine vehicles cost more initially, but do tend to last longer and depreciate less. However for the retiree, unless you intend covering a high mileage, the initial purchase cost makes them less economical. But diesels are more suitable for towing caravans, which is why I have one.

Taxis and buses use diesel engines due to the high mileages covered.

An LPG conversion on a petrol engine will more or less halve your fuel bill, but the cost of the conversion may make it prohibitive. Some conversions cost over £2,000, but others can be as low as £600. See: http://www.leedslpg.co.uk/lpg .

Another downside to LPG is that part of your boot space is taken up by the additional fuel tank.

An electric or part electric powered vehicle could certainly be the most economical option per mile, but an *all electric* vehicle will have a very limited range between charges. And in all cases right now the initial high purchase price counteracts the fuel savings unless your annual mileage is enormous.

Having discovered the true cost of owning and running a car, you may decide to look into other options, which we'll cover shortly.

For me actually getting rid of my car would involve extensive surgery, but it does make sense to look at the other options, even just to keep the costs down a little.

Servicing

The cost of car maintenance for essentially the same service can vary enormously. Common sense might tell you that you will get the best service from the manufacturers main agents and that you should stay away from small time 'cowboys'. As a generalisation this may be true, **but** the main agents charges are often outrageous.

I used to do all of my own servicing back in the days of plugs and points etc., but since the introduction of electronic engine management (ECU's) and special tools for just about everything, there's very little that I can now do myself.

Personally I use a local *'work from home'* mechanic who is good, reliable and economical and I trust him 100%. Sure there are cowboys out there, but there's just as many crap main agents! So my advice would be to find a good low cost local mechanic who has been recommended by your friends. But do have your vehicle serviced and cam belt changed at the recommended intervals (it's false economy not to) unless you are going for the *banger* option.

Accidents

I'd like to say otherwise, but unfortunately with the amount of vehicles on our roads, accidents are inevitable. Although many accidents can be avoided; even if you drive perfectly in complete accordance with the Highway Code for the whole of your life, you cannot prevent someone running into the back of you, as has happened to me on numerous occasions.

In the event of an accident and in order to hopefully minimise your losses and protect your no claims bonus and 'non fault' status, you must take the correct action. Obviously, you must comply with all the legal requirements such as: stopping; warning other traffic; calling the emergency services if anyone is injured etc., but beyond all this, if you want to minimise your losses, take note of the following:

- If possible get details of any independent witnesses who can help confirm the other parties fault;
- Take photos of the scene *before* anything is moved;
- Make a note of all other vehicles make / model, colour and registration details;
- Ask for insurance details from other parties;
- Make sure you know who was driving the other vehicle and if there were any passengers;
- Ask for names, addresses and telephone numbers of all other parties involved;
- Give your details to other parties involved;
- If possible try and get the other party to admit liability and sign a statement to this effect - but if they agree to

this they would be totally bonkers, so don't hold your breath;

- Never admit liability yourself, even if you think you may have been at fault, as things aren't always what they seem;

- Do not waste time arguing with the other party - this will achieve nothing apart from raising your blood pressure;

- Make a note of the exact time, weather and visibility;

- Note if any vehicle was using headlights;

- Note if any vehicle sounded their horn or flashed their lights or signalled etc.;

- Note road markings and signs and take photographs if possible;

- Take measurements of the road widths, so that the exact location of the collision can be identified on your insurance claims form;

- Contact your insurance company as soon as possible.

Obviously, the above is an awful lot to remember, especially when you are stressed out, so I have created an accident report form, which you'd be wise to copy and keep in your vehicle - you'll be glad you did! This can be downloaded from my website at: http://martinwoodward.net/accident_form.html free of charge.

In addition to the above, when you get home, it will be useful to get a Google overhead shot of the road(s) involved and make a copy of this (using 'screen capture' or similar). This will be most useful when making out your report for the insurance company and enable you to make scale drawings of the event, for both immediately before and at the point of impact. And remember the better the report, the more likely it will be believed by the insurance company - and it's *them* who matter!

If the accident is deemed 'knock for knock' (in other words neither party can be held fully to blame) this is just as bad as a *'fault'* accident and you will lose your no claims bonus and excess.

You have to *prove* the other party to be at fault in order to keep your valuable fault free status and sometimes this is difficult.

Following are a few typical accidents where it's fairly easy to prove who's at fault:

- Waiting to enter a roundabout;

- Pulling out of a side road;

- Reversing into a main road.

But these are virtually impossible to prove without witnesses or video evidence:

- Collision at traffic lights - how do you prove what colour they were?

- Damage occurring when your vehicle is parked (unless you happen to see the event);

- Side collision in the middle of a roundabout through someone *'drifting'* out of their lane into yours. They could simply argue that you *'drifted'*.

In all these cases check to see if there are any CCTV recordings of the event available which could prove your claim. Or better still fit a windscreen video camera to your vehicle; these are now available for little over £20 from eBay and are highly recommended.

There was a time when the police would attend all road traffic accidents however minor, but these days they are simply not interested unless someone is injured.

Hiring Cars

Depending on your age, experience and where you live, hiring a car when you need it can be a real and economical option. For instance if you live in London and don't have anywhere to park a car, owning one can actually be a liability and constant worry.

One of my son's once ran a pub in Islington and although he paid for residents parking he often had to park 20 minutes or more away from his residence and lost count of how many times it got broken into. And ironically, while he was there he hardly ever used it, so had he hired a vehicle for the few journeys that he needed to make he would have achieved a considerable saving.

Also *always* check the insurance details with regards to excess charges. Time and time again I've seen hire companies advertise *'all inclusive'* insurance only to find that there is a £500 - £2000 excess in the event of an accident and this amount will simply be taken from your credit card (which you will have unknowingly agreed to). Nearly all hire companies now do this but most also offer an additional insurance to cover this amount, but this is usually a very expensive daily charge.

You'd also be wise to take photos of all existing damage and have the company's agent sign a document agreeing this, as you may well get charged for it when you return the car.

Be particularly careful if hiring a car abroad (especially Spain, Portugal and Cyprus), some operatives are out and out confidence tricksters (especially with the excess payments) - be warned! And in the event of an accident abroad it will almost certainly be deemed to be your fault whatever happens, so extra vigilance is required! - Take your windscreen video cam with you!

Car Sharing Schemes

There are two types of 'car sharing' arrangements:

1.   Where you enter an arrangement with another driver who works near you and share the motoring costs;

2.   Where you join a consortium and can hire a car for as little as two hours perhaps to do your shopping etc.

Both of these arrangements can be hugely beneficial although as you are retired you should no longer need the first option.

Google search 'car sharing' for your locality and see what comes up!

Make Full Use of Your Bus Pass

The OAP bus pass is a blessing indeed. You would be advised to make full use of it even if you have a car, as it may not last.

Although your bus pass can be used Nationwide (between 09:30 and 23:00 weekdays, all day at weekends and holidays). There may also be additional local benefits - check your area.

For further intercity travel, having an OAP rail card and booking at the correct time can almost certainly work out cheaper (for two people and certainly for one) than taking the car - and far less stressful.

But of course I know there are other factors to consider such as where you live in relation to a station and of course times and convenience etc.

Cycling

Depending on where you live and where you want to go to cycling can be a fantastic way of getting around and naturally it's free after the initial investment and parking is never a problem. It also helps keep you fit.

But unfortunately the big downside is the danger from other traffic. Another absolutely crazy waste of public money in the last few years is all the 'cycle lanes' created which are nothing more than paint in the road, offering the cyclists no protection or segregation whatsoever. Clearly the object of the exercise was simply to be able to quote a statistic - "We have created X amount of cycle lanes during our time in power!" *Complete bollocks - they just wasted a load of paint!*

The only cycle lanes that are any good are the ones that segregate the cyclists from the traffic as they do in Holland and Belgium. Many of our 'cycle lanes' are for buses as well - I mean like they really go together well, don't they?

My advice is only use cycling as a means of transport if you can do so safely and if you do, always wear a helmet and something bright as well as the appropriate lights in bad weather and at night and watch out for pot holes and tram lines etc.

But beyond being a means of transport, cycling can be great in rural areas where there are dedicated cycle tracks which are completely off road, such as the Tissington Trail and Derwent Valley in Derbyshire. No doubt there are hundreds more in other areas and some near you, many of which also hire out bikes.

Walking

Walking has to be the most cost effective way of getting from A to B and is something that we should all do more of for the sake of our health and wealth.

Of course it's only useful for relatively short journeys and the weather is often an issue.

If walking though rough terrain invest in the correct shoes / boots for the job and perhaps a stick. I have a stick which I used to take with me in Cyprus as a protection from snakes and scorpions. I doesn't get used for the same purpose here, but I still like it.

If venturing out in ice be sure to have some ice grips fitted to your shoes as you don't want to break any bones. These are available very cheaply on eBay and they've saved me a few falls.

Motability

If you or your partner are disabled, you may be entitled to a free car via the *motability* scheme. If you qualify, this has to be the most cost effective way of running a car as you'll not have to worry about tax / insurance, repairs or accidents etc. - just fuel and tyres.

I've known single parents become eligible for this valuable benefit because their kids are too fat to walk to school! Yet many genuine pensioners are not claiming their entitlement. My mother was definitely entitled to this but never claimed it due to pride!

See: http://www.motability.co.uk for more details.

Banks / Credit Cards

It's a fact of life now that we are all compelled to have a bank account, whereas in days gone by that we all remember too well, they were only an option. And gone are the good old fashioned bank accounts that we all know about from the 60's and before. They're a distant memory that will never return.

I don't need to say anything here to discredit the banks, they do a good enough job themselves virtually on a daily basis! So now I'm thinking of something good to say about them .... no .... nothing's coming, ... I'll have to leave that one!

To be honest as long you have a non fee paying - no frills account with an overdraft facility that suits your needs, it doesn't make much difference which one you're with as they're just about all as bad as one another. I've been with the same bank for 40 years on the basis of - 'better the devil you know!'

Recently I was thinking about changing to the Co-op on ethical grounds - enough said!

If you've been talked into opening one of those accounts where you pay a monthly fee for certain benefits, you'd probably be wise to change it to a basic non fee paying account - but make sure that they don't charge you for arranging an overdraft facility. They all have a nasty habit of inventing a whole host of fees that never used to exist. That's another reason I'm staying put!

The fee paying accounts are only worth it if you genuinely use the benefits regularly and they are not available cheaper elsewhere. And of course always read the small print.

No doubt your pension / income will be paid directly into your account on a weekly, monthly or fortnightly basis and many of your outgoings will be paid out by direct debit or standing order and of course you will make cash withdrawals.

Managing your account correctly so that there is always enough funds available to cover outgoings is essential which is where a small overdraft facility can be useful as long as it's used correctly. But if you enter the unauthorised overdraft area even for 1p for one day, outrageous fees and charges will inevitably follow, bumping your account further into the red ready for even more charges and creating a never ending spiral of debt. But you should know all this anyway and hopefully are sensible enough to have a good home accounts system in place which you update regularly.

Direct Debits / Standing Orders / CPA's

Direct debits, standing orders and CPA's are all ways of making regular payments from your bank account or credit card(s) and its very important that you know the difference between them.

A standing order is an arrangement which you set up with company or organisation whereby you agree to pay a fixed (unchanging) amount into their account on a regular basis (per month, per year etc.). You can cancel this anytime by contacting your bank.

Most standing orders are being replaced by direct debits which are similar but the recipient has the right to alter the amount. Typically these are used by utility providers where your monthly bill amount may vary. All good responsible companies would advise you a few days before the payment is due so that you can ensure that funds are available. These can also be cancelled by you at any time.

Now the CPA (continuous payment authority) have caused immense grief in the past as these are payments to companies via your credit card. In the past in order to stop these you had to contact the company, who were often conveniently for them uncontactable, but recently the rules have changed giving you the right to cancel these via your credit card company.

Actually, these are regularly used by confidence tricksters around the world and I briefly fell afoul of one myself, which I'll outline here to warn you.

This started with an internet advert within a *respectable* site which offered a free sample of a miracle face cream, but the sting was that they wanted about 90p postage. No great amount, but of course to give them the 90p I had to give my credit card details and tick the terms and condition box which no one reads. But within these terms and conditions was an agreement to carry on buying more jars of this cream for £50 per month until cancelled.

Now we never actually received the cream, and the first I noticed was that they'd taken £50 from my credit card. I immediately notified my card company who informed me that (at that time) they could not cancel the agreement and put me onto the company (who they could contact but I couldn't). I explained to them that I hadn't received any cream and didn't want any anyway and asked them to refund my card. They said that the cream was on the way and they couldn't cancel it.

Well, we still never received the cream (which actually was lucky), so I got back on to the credit card company by which time another £50 was taken. As it was then considered fraud the credit card company were able to act and refunded me both amounts, but even they couldn't stop the CPA without cancelling the card and issuing me with a new one.

But now you have the right to cancel CPA's without asking the recipient, but some banks haven't grasped this point - so beware. My advice is never issue a CPA, always read the small print and be extra suspicious of companies who only want very small amounts from you as they are obviously just after your details!

Withdrawing Cash

When withdrawing cash from ATM machines, firstly make sure that you are not being charged for the transaction. At most supermarket and bank ATM's you will not be charged a fee for debit card withdrawals - that's money that is in your bank account. But if you are using a credit card there will almost certainly be a charge from the credit card company.

Always be vigilant when using these machines and remember that you never know what a thief or confidence trickster looks like. And even when you've withdrawn the cash remember you could still be a target. Unfortunately some of us oldies are very vulnerable in such circumstances. I don't want to make you paranoid, just aware. Problems only occur in a very small minority of cases, but if it does happen to you, it could be devastating. Possibly a slightly safer alternative is to get *cash back* when buying shopping using your debit card.

For me personally, it's never a problem as I always have the wife on guard ready to give any suspicious characters a good hand bagging!

Contactless Card Payment

Now here's something that even if you're incredibly astute you might not know.

Most new credit and debit cards automatically come with the contactless feature included. If this is included on your card you will see the following symbol in the corner of your card:

In short this means that you can use this type of card for small payments (usually £20 or less) on any payment machine displaying the symbol shown below.

All you have to do is tap the card on the machine - done - no pin - no messing - very convenient!

But it also means that if anyone steals or finds your card they could have an absolute beano at your expense without even having your pin number!

AND furthermore, London Transport has recently started accepting these in addition to the contactless Oyster card. Sure you don't need it, you've got a bus pass, but if you get your wallet or purse containing the card too close to the machine, it's going to take your money anyway! If this happens you can actually get your money back from London Transport, but do you need the grief?

And of course the fraudsters are onto this as well and have invented a device that captures your cards contactless details just by rubbing passed your handbag etc. Then they're on a spending spree. Sure, they can only spend up to £20 a time but they can do it an awful lot of times!

Now, being a bit concerned about this, I contacted my bank and simply asked them who pays if all this goes wrong. The reply was a load of gobbledegook referring me to various URL's (web pages) with supposedly the relevant information.

I asked them again, "All I want to know is who pays you or me? It's a simple question requiring a one word answer." Again they sidestepped and sent me more gobbledegook!

To be fair if your card is stolen, after a few successive unusual contactless payments, the pin number would be asked for and the card would then be declined, but who pays up to that point is unclear to me.

I actually use this feature quite a lot, mainly in the post office and I do find it convenient. But if you are concerned about this, you could request that your bank and / or credit card company remove the feature.

You can also buy aluminium card wallets to prevent thieves and London Transport from scanning your card; these are available on eBay for about £4.

Credit Cards

Credit cards are both very bad and very good according to how you use them. They are very bad because:

- Their interest rates are generally appalling if you don't pay them off *in full* each month;
- If you are unwise it's all too easy to enter a spiral of debt;
- The CPAs are not a good idea (as mentioned previously).

But they can be very good for the following reasons:

- They can be extremely useful in an emergency (when on holiday abroad etc.);
- Some offer interest free credit on credit transfers (although there is generally a 3% or more set up charge for this);
- Some offer an interest free period for purchases;
- Some even offer cash back on your usage, it's usually only about 1%, but even that could be enough to buy the wife a diamond ring and magnifying glass enabling her to see it!;
- They give you additional security for major purchases, in the fact that you can seek a refund from the credit card company for faulty goods, or bankrupt holiday provider etc.

So in a nutshell, they are ideal for major purchases or booking holidays etc., as long as you pay them off IN FULL within the interest free credit time.

Or they can also be used to help clear a debt by transferring to one offering interest free credit for a limited period (usually 6 months but sometimes more). But remember there will be a transfer fee for this service - typically 3%.

In the past many card companies offered interest free transfers with no charges and I once bought a house using three credit cards and bounced the balance around at the end of the interest free periods. But unfortunately, now the transfer fees make such games less viable.

And again when taking out a new card make sure you do it via *quidco* or *topcashback*. Only recently I received a £40 cash back payment for applying for a credit card that I don't particularly want and will probably never use! *If you do just this and nothing else you will recoup the cost of this book many times over!*

Borrowing Money

Hopefully, you are in a position where you don't need to borrow any money, but of course everyone's circumstances are different. So here we'll look at the following:

- Authorised Overdrafts;
- Unauthorised Overdrafts;
- Payday Loans;
- Log Book Loans;
- Loan Sharks;
- Pawn Brokers;
- Personal Loans;
- Equity Release;
- Hire Purchase;
- Lease Purchase;
- Personal Contract Purchase;
- Interest Free Credit;
- Mail Order Catalogues;
- Credit Cards.

Authorised Overdrafts

As mentioned previously, these can be a great asset simply to cover you for very short lengths of time, if a direct debit comes out of your bank account at an inconvenient time. If used correctly, the interest on these should be less than a pound a month. But if you get to the situation whereby your account is continually using this facility and you get near or into the unauthorised overdraft situation, then you need to take immediate action to get things straight.

Unauthorised Overdrafts

Basically an unauthorised overdraft is stealing and you should never get into this situation. If you do you will be charged fees for getting into the situation, further fees if your bank has to decline direct debits as well as interest which is comparable with payday loans.

See 'dealing with debt' - shortly.

Payday Loans

If you borrowed £1 from a well known payday loan company (no names mentioned) and didn't pay anything back, in 20 years you would owe them £22,338,759,771,594.20, that's 22 trillion, 338 billion, 759 million, 771 thousand, 594 pounds and 20 pence! That is more than 10 times the countries national debt! Perhaps you should just settle for 10p! This is how outrageous their interest rates are. How payday loans have managed to legally come into being is beyond my comprehension, but clearly there's an awful lot of stupid people around. If you can't make ends meet this month, you won't next month either and taking a payday loan will only make the situation worse.

Payday loans are the rocky road to self destruction and anyone who thinks they desperately need one should seek debt counselling without delay.

There's only one circumstance where I recommend a payday loan and that is to borrow the £700 fee to declare yourself bankrupt, so that they legally can't get it back! But even then make sure you borrow it before you make the application so that they are listed as a creditor!

Log Book Loans

A log book loan is a loan using your car as collateral. Usually the interest is not quite as bad as payday loans, but basically these are just as stupid. At least they keep the repossession men in jobs!

Loan Sharks

Loan sharks are illegal money lenders who predominantly prey on the poor and vulnerable. Their interest rates are in line with pay day loans (or worse) and will lead to ruin. These individuals or organisations are actually worse than pay day loans as they often frog march their victims to the cash points on the day they receive their benefits and take everything from them. Also threats, intimidation and violence can be involved, and even going bankrupt won't stop them. Clearly these people need locking up!

If you know of any loan sharks you can report them anonymously at https://www.gov.uk/report-loan-shark .

Pawn Brokers

Using pawn brokers has been going on for generations by the financially inept. No doubt many family heirlooms and precious gifts have been lost this way.

'Cash Converters' are a modern day equivalent.

Personal Loans

The interest on a personal loan could basically be anything from very reasonable to outrageous and may be 'unsecured' or 'secured' on your house - putting your home at risk in the event of default. Generally speaking, the only place to go would be a bank or building society. But even then check the rate of interest (APR) carefully and make sure that you know exactly how much you are borrowing over what period of time and how much you are paying back. Also check early redemption fees should you wish to repay early.

But personally speaking at our time of life, taking out loans is not a good idea especially for things like holidays or cars etc. My view is: if you can't afford it don't buy it!

Equity Release

Equity release has been dealt with previously, and is probably your best option for raising capital, or rather releasing some of the value from your home which you've worked for. But due to the set up fees this is not advised for relatively small sums.

Hire Purchase

Hire Purchase (HP) is a loan secured on the item purchased, which could be a car or furniture etc. Due to clauses in the agreements whereby the buyer has the right to return the goods after a certain amount of payments, it's not used as much these days.

The car sellers now tend to prefer the Lease Purchase or Personal Contract Purchase and furniture sellers generally use unsecured personal loans.

Lease Purchase (mainly for vehicles)

Lease purchase is similar to HP, but normally the deposit is paid at the end of the term rather than at the beginning and can be anything from 10% to 50% of the purchase price of the vehicle. This is known as the *'residual'* value (payment). When this point is reached, you can either pay the large final payment and thereby secure ownership of the vehicle, or relinquish the vehicle back to the finance company.

This is how car dealers can offer 'no deposit' and 'low monthly payments' - with the hidden *sting* at the end!

And to make matters worse there's often an agreed annual mileage and if you go over this figure and wish to relinquish the vehicle, there will be a penalty for each mile over the agreed limit.

As with the HP the vehicle is the security for the loan and as such you would be required to insure the vehicle fully comprehensively.

Personal Contract Purchase (mainly for vehicles)

The 'personal contract purchase' is certainly the *nastiest* of all the legal vehicle finance arrangements and probably the most used. It's also the most confusing and often purchasers enter this arrangement without fully understanding the consequences.

This arrangement is more or less a combination of the Hire Purchase and Lease Purchase deals and involves the following:

- Initial deposit (typically 10% but could be more or less);
- An agreed amount of monthly payments (typically 24, 36 or 48);
- A large single final payment to secure ownership which is known as the *'minimum guaranteed future value'* (MGFV) or *'balloon payment'*. This figure is agreed at the time of *'purchase'*;
- The purchaser has the option to return the vehicle to the finance company or pay the final agreed payment.

Similar to the HP and Lease Purchase arrangements, the buyer (or rather *'hirer'*) would be obliged to insure the vehicle fully comprehensively for the duration.

There may also be mileage and possible maintenance conditions and of course interest rates could vary tremendously.

But basically this arrangement enables dealers to sell vehicles to people who can't really afford to buy them and can lead to devastating consequences. *Enter this arrangement at your peril - you've been warned!*

Interest Free Credit

If it suits your budget, then genuine interest free credit is fine, although interest will almost certainly be hidden into the deal by increasing the cost of the goods purchased. This is really nothing more than an unsecured personal loan often used by furniture companies.

This can be a sensible way of spreading the cost of certain furniture items that you will invariably need every so often. We recently bought a dining suite this way from DFS with 3 years interest free. But if you want to take advantage of this, you better be quick as their sale ends 5:00 pm on Sunday!

Another common type of 'interest free' credit is used by companies like Argos who sometimes offer items with 9 months interest free credit, but with a bit of a sting in the tail if you're unaware. Basically, you don't have to pay anything until the due date and then the full amount is payable, but if you go one day over, then interest will be added at credit card rates for the whole period. Obviously they are hoping that you forget and fall into their clutches.

I actually bought my laptop from Argos for a good price with this deal, but I split the amount into eight equal instalments to make sure that it was paid in full before the due date. And I couldn't have got a better price anywhere even for cash, so the deal worked nicely in my favour.

Mail Order Catalogues

Generally speaking the majority of goods that are sold via mail order catalogues are grossly overpriced and then to rub salt into the wounds they charge crazy interest on top. Do you really need to suffer like this?

Credit Cards

Dealt with in the last chapter. These are great to have as a financial tool, but get into their debt at your peril!

Dealing with Debt

The best way of dealing with debt, is not to get there in the first place, but at your age you should already know this.

But it's a sad fact that there are an awful lot of OAP's in this miserable situation. If you are one of them, then how you should deal with this depends on:

- The severity of the situation; and
- Your assets.

The first thing is to face the problem squarely and honestly to find out *exactly* how much you owe and to whom.

The usual scenario of how people get into these situations is by borrowing from several different sources so that the situation doesn't look so bad when you look at them individually. But this is nothing more than burying your head in the sand.

So add the whole lot up and get the real full picture. And don't let anyone talk you into consolidating the debt into 'one simple monthly payment which will also give you a further £5,000 to spend as you wish' - this is the way of the complete fool!

The next thing to do is to work out your disposable income. That is what's left after paying all your essential outgoings like food, heating, council tax etc.

Then whatever is left over is the amount that you will have available for paying off your debts plus any assets that you may have.

At this point if you feel that you are able to deal with the situation without further help, the next thing to do is to write to your creditors and explain the situation and ask for the interest to be frozen so that you can then make an offer of repayment which you can sensibly afford - then stick to it and hopefully learn your lesson.

Most companies will be reasonable as they know that if you eventually go bankrupt, they will get nothing.

If the situation is so bad that you are unable to deal with it yourself then you must seek some independent counselling immediately - do not let the situation spiral further out of control which it will if not dealt with.

See: http://www.nationaldebtline.co.uk .

You will find that there are several avenues open to you such as:

- DMP - Debt Management Plan;
- IVA - Individual Voluntary Arrangement;
- DRO - Debt Relief Order (fees £90);
- Bankruptcy (fees £700);
- Offer Full & Final Settlement (a reduced figure);
- AO Administration Order;
- Ask to Have the debt Written Off;
- Consolidation Loan (at a suitable interest rate).

Which is best for you will be determined by the amount of the debt, your assets and your income.

If you own your own home, this will certainly be at risk whichever option you choose. In this event an equity release mortgage might be your best option - but you must seek specialist advice.

If you live in social housing with no assets, actually the solution is easier as your debtors will have less (if anything) to take from you and are consequently more likely to settle more easily.

Gambling

Over £42 billion per year is lost in the UK by those who have fallen prey to gambling - a shocking statistic! And clearly the majority of this is taken from the poor, as the huge majority of gambling dens (betting shops) are in the poorest areas. This has become far worse since the arrival of the fixed odds betting terminals (FOBTs), introduced by the last labour government supposedly the party who looks after the interests of the poor!

Make no mistake about it, gambling:

- Destroys marriages;
- Ruins lives;
- Causes poverty;
- Is the cause of many crimes (theft and violence);
- Is just one step up from drug dealing;
- Is paid for indirectly by every decent citizen.

Shame on the scum who run these organizations; shame on the people who work for them; shame on those who accept their advertising; shame on those who rent them the premises; and shame on the governments who allow it!

And sadly you don't even need to step outside to do it thanks to the introduction of online gambling, just enter your credit card details and give them your money - you don't stand a chance! *"Join the fun!"* Sure, they might throw you a few crumbs, but this is just to get you hooked in further - the same tactics as the drug dealers.

If you are addicted to gambling (and make no mistake, the FOBTs are cleverly designed to get you addicted), re-take charge of your life by seeking help - see: http://www.gamcare.org.uk or call 0808 8020 133 (free) - do it now!

So what about the lotto and premium bonds? They're gambling too!

Yes, but passive gambling is far different to serious addictive gambling - not in the same league. Although even the lotto in extreme cases can be addictive, but by and large a quid or two here and there is nothing more than a bit of fun with the proceeds going to a good cause (allegedly). And with premium bonds you are retaining your stake but gambling with the interest.

Even a night out at the 'dogs' or 'Bingo' (not online Bingo) can be 'entertainment' rather than addictive gambling, it just depends on how far you take it. But if you have an addictive personality, it's probably best to keep away from all temptations.

Personally my 'gambling' goes no further than the premium bonds. I learnt my lesson many years ago when I once lost half a crown on a 'one arm bandit' on Brighton pier!

What the Dickens 2?

Now I know that you can make figures say anything and I know you're not a fool, so please don't take this too literally. It's clearly just *an* example.

But basically by following the guidelines herein in order to increase your income and / or reduce your expenditure I'm confident that everyone can produce some improvement to their current circumstances.

Ok, so the example here's an improvement of the hypothetical example which I showed in the first chapter.

Firstly here's the revised income. Due to their income level, all the time they were eligible for the guaranteed pension credit and the savings credit as shown below. This alone has made a dramatic improvement to their circumstances.

And as they are claiming the guaranteed credit, this automatically entitles them to a 100% reduction in their council tax bill further improving their situation.

Mr & Mrs Clever Income		
	Before	**After**
State Pension	£180.90	£180.90
Private Pension	£25.00	£25.00
Pension Credit (guaranteed)	£0.00	£20.60
Pension Credit (savings)	£0.00	£8.34
Additional Earnings	£0.00	£10.00
Winter Fuel Allnce	£3.85	£3.85
Total Income	**£209.75**	**£248.69**

In addition, Mr Clever now has a part time job earning £10 per week doing a bit of dog walking.

Now moving onto the expenditure, you will see as you look down the following list that savings have been made through:

- Changing to a better gas / electric supplier;

- Installing water saving devices and thereby reducing metered costs;

- Switching to a more competitive telephone / internet provider;

- Only insuring essential white goods;

- Reducing clothes allowance by buying quality hardly used bargains at charity shops and online;

- Christmas budget has been reduced to a mere £500 for the year - still not bad;

- The window cleaner has been sacked. You can buy devices to clean upstairs windows without climbing ladders;

- Incidentals, holidays and emergency repairs have remained the same;

- Entertainment has been reduced to £5 per week, but you make your choice - this can be increased at the expense of the holiday;

- Dental / optical and pet insurance have been eliminated due to the guaranteed pension credit;

- House insurance has been reduced simply due to searching for a better price;

- Life insurance remains the same as it's not worth changing;

- Pet insurance has been eliminated due to the PDSA.

Mr & Mrs Clever Expenditure		
	Before	**After**
Council Tax	£25.51	£0.00
Heat / Light	£25.00	£20.00
Water	£10.00	£7.00
Groceries	£94.40	£68.00
Telephone / Internet	£10.00	£5.50
TV Licence	£2.50	£2.50
White Goods Insurance	£4.00	£2.00
White Goods Replacement	£3.00	£3.00
Motoring	£57.00	£36.50
Clothes	£20.00	£10.00
Xmas	£20.00	£10.00
Window cleaner	£2.50	£0.00
Incidental	£10.00	£10.00
Holidays	£25.00	£25.00
Emergency Repairs	£10.00	£10.00
Entertainment	£20.00	£5.00
Dental / Optical	£2.00	£0.00
Life Insurance	£5.00	£5.00
Pet Insurance	£4.00	£0.00
House Insurance	£4.00	£3.00
Total	**£353.91**	**£222.50**

Now we'll look at the more detailed analysis of the groceries. Everyone spends their money differently, so to create a *'one size fits all'* scenario is impossible. Obviously you may not buy some of the items but may buy others not included, so please take this with a *pinch of salt*.

Savings have been made as follows:

- Firstly you'll notice that I've reduced the papers from £5.40 per week to 90p. This based on buying the Daily Mail and Mail on Sunday on a continual basis, which equates to £5.40 per week at today's prices or £2,808 over a ten year period. Personally, I can think of much better ways of spending £2,808 in ten years rather than allowing myself to be subjected to the propaganda and mental manipulation of the newspapers. You may well think otherwise and of course it's your choice. So I've reduced this to 90p per week by buying only the Saturday copy which also includes a free comprehensive TV guide which seems a fair deal to me. Free newspaper can be obtained my nipping on a bus for couple of stops or go to the local library or find them free online at http://www.wrx.zen.co.uk;

Groceries		
	Before	**After**
Papers	£5.40	£0.90
Bread	£5.00	£4.50
Meat	£5.00	£4.50
Vegetables	£5.00	£4.50
Cereals	£5.00	£4.50
Tea / Coffee	£2.00	£1.80
Milk	£3.00	£2.70
eggs	£3.00	£2.70
Cheese	£2.00	£1.80
Beans	£2.00	£1.80
Soup	£2.00	£1.80
Fish	£5.00	£4.50
Cigarettes	£30.00	£15.00
Booze	£10.00	£8.00
Washing Powder	£3.00	£2.70
Soap / Toiletries	£3.00	£2.70
medicines	£2.00	£1.80
Cleaning stuff	£2.00	£1.80
Total	**£94.40**	**£68.00**

- Now the rest of the stuff I've reduced by 10% simply by being a more astute shopper with the exception of the cigarettes and booze;

- Personally I don't smoke or drink and am very glad of this, but I know that it's easy to say *just don't do it* and save the money. I have smoked very heavily in the past, so I know how difficult it is to stop, in fact I went through the pain of *'giving up'* several times a week before I eventually just stopped! But if you've been a smoker for 40 plus years, I would not recommend going cold turkey as your body will be so used to the chemicals that the sudden shock might finish you off; - gradually cutting down might be better, if you want to. Anyway, I've reduced the cigarette bill to £15.00 per week by changing to roll ups which offer better value for money;

- I've reduced the booze spending to £8.00 per week by looking for the bargains.

Now we'll look in more details at what improvements we've made to the motoring expenses as shown below.

- Immediately you'll notice that I've halved the fuel bill, by making better use of the free bus pass. And of course fuel is always purchased at the cheapest local price. Every penny per litre equates to £1.50 per 1000 miles if your vehicle does 30 mpg - no great amount I know but sometimes the price variation can be as much as 5p per litre which is £75 per 10,000 miles. It all adds up!;

- Road tax unfortunately can't be altered other than changing to a lower emission vehicle;

- The MOT and breakdown cover have both been reduced as a result of searching out the best price;

- Car washing has been reduced to nil as if you are prepared to pay someone to wash your car, you shouldn't need this book!;

- Parking fees have been reduced to nil by using the buses to go anywhere where there's a parking fee;

- Insurance has been reduced by effective use of comparison websites;

- Servicing and depreciation have both been reduced as a result of lower mileage.

Motoring		
	Before	After
Fuel	£18.00	£9.00
Road Tax	£3.00	£3.00
Mot	£1.00	£0.50
Breakdown Cover	£1.50	£1.00
Car Washing	£3.00	£0.00
Parking	£0.50	£0.00
Insurance	£4.00	£3.00
Servicing	£6.00	£5.00
Depreciation	£20.00	£15.00
Total	£57.00	£36.50

The final result is shown below. As you can see the £144.16 per week deficit has been turned into a comfortable £26.19 credit enabling Mr McCawber to sleep soundly in his grave!

Mr & Mrs Clever Balance		
	Before	After
Total Weekly Income	£209.75	£248.69
Total Weekly Expenditure	£353.91	£222.50
Balance	-£144.16	£26.19

And note that they still:

- Eat, smoke and drink;

- Heat their property;

- Run a car; and

- Go on holiday!

And this doesn't include any additional 'cash back' income earned through 'quidco' etc.

Everything comes at a cost and how you decide to spend your limited funds is your choice. Looking again at the main expenditure chart you'll see at a glance that beyond food, motoring is the biggest expense, so a particular close eye needs to be kept on this item.

But the key to making it all work is **budgeting** correctly and consistently!

Things You Can Do for Free or Almost

As you drive down from Kathikas to Peyia in Cyprus, in the summer mornings there is often a dense cloud half way down the hill. But you would be mistaken if you think that bad weather is on the way. I don't know where it eventually condenses, but it won't rain until October.

The cloud is caused by the hundreds of swimming pools owned predominantly by British ex pats. A few are happy with their lot, at least for the time being. Others are desperate to sell up and come home as they can no longer afford to live there - we were lucky, we enjoyed our time there, then got real with our price and sold at the right time - before the main exodus. The really unfortunate ones have had to abandon their properties and return empty handed to live in rented accommodation. Others, who can still afford to be there are literally drinking themselves to death - through boredom and alcohol addiction. And the same thing is happening in Spain. *Such is the dream!*

During my life's journey, I've been blessed with both being reasonably well off (although not *rich*), as well as experiencing times when I've had to scratch around for the next meal. Unsurprisingly, I've concluded that having *enough* money for your needs and a bit left over is definitely better than the contrary.

But I've also concluded that money will most certainly not bring lasting happiness - the two are not connected. Looking back over my life, many of my happiest times were when I had no money.

Sure, if you have stacks of the stuff, you can do more things. but thankfully there's still many activities that you can do for nothing or almost nothing rather than just stagnating in front of the TV.

Here's just a few examples:

- Walking Groups;
- Go to University;
- Lunch Clubs;
- Learn Meditation or Tai Chi or Yoga;
- Photography;
- Libraries;
- Museums / Art Galleries;
- Communal Gardening;
- Go fishing;
- Go for a Picnic;
- Go Treasure Hunting;
- Go 'Miniature' Sailing;
- Join a Drama Group;
- Learn a Musical Instrument;
- Help Others;
- Simply Socialise with Friends!

Walking Groups

Every area has walking groups for all levels of fitness. And this can be a great way to socialise as well as keeping fit without burning yourself out. Check out the notice boards in your local library or doctors surgery.

I recently picked up some free leaflets with local walks at our doctors.

Go to University

The University of the Third Age is a charitable organisation operating throughout the UK and is run *by* retirees *for* retirees and offers a whole range of possibilities for your life's enrichment.

You could become involved by being a student or teacher or both. See: http://www.u3a.org.uk or call 020 8466 6139 to see what's available in your area.

Lunch Clubs

Lunch Clubs and coffee mornings are often run be local churches. A great way to get out and socialise regardless of your faith (or non faith).

Meditation, Yoga or Tai Chi

Meditation can be incredibly good for you on every level, physically, mentally and spiritually and needn't be connected to any religion or faith. You don't need to tie yourself in knots, just get comfortable and watch your breath go in and out - easy, and the benefits can be enormous. See my site: http://www.deep-relaxation.co.uk for more information where you will also find some freebies to help get you going.

Yoga or Tai Chi are both gentle ways of keeping fit and are both ideally suited for OAP's. Generally there will be a small fee for learning these as they involve the instructors time and premises - a fair exchange!

Photography

There was a time when getting into photography was very expensive, mainly due to the costs of films and developing. But with the introduction of digital photography most of these costs have vanished. Even a small digital camera costing less than £50 can take some pretty good shots. But if you were to invest in a more expensive SLR (single lens reflex) with a range of lenses the potential is endless. Then just snap away for free, store the images on your computer and print out the good ones as and when you see fit.

Photography naturally can be tied in with other activities, like walking etc. And don't worry about running out of subjects, if you get into 'macro' you can make a little bug look like a monster! And every tree, animal and skyline is a masterpiece waiting to be captured!

Libraries

Libraries offer a whole wealth of knowledge for books, music and films. And also as mentioned previously, in many cases you can gain access to the internet for free.

With the need for cutting public spending I fear for many of the local libraries as there is no charge to use the facilities yet they must cost an awful lot to run. Use them while we've still got them as they may not last!

Museums & Art Galleries

Similar to libraries, museums and art galleries in many cases offer a free service which may not stay free indefinitely. Enjoy them while you can!

Communal Gardening

As mentioned previously, many local gardening groups are popping up just about everywhere. You'll probably find details of one close to you in your local library.

These are a brilliant idea. Basically, you share the work and share the rewards. And of course at the same time you will make new friends and keep fit.

Go Fishing

Apparently fishing is the most popular hobby by a long way. Nothing else comes near it. I see this as a form of meditation - a way of turning off and completely forgetting your problems.

Personally I'd rather meditate and leave the fish in peace, but everyone to their own!

Picnics

Rediscover the joys of having of an old fashioned picnic in the park with sandwiches, crisps and a flask, which would now cost you far more than a tenner for two if you went to the park cafe. Or maybe do it French style with a fresh baguette, cheese and vino and you can even end up with a game of *boules* afterwards - *très magnifique!*

Over the years I've eaten in some pretty fancy places which I'm thankful for; at least I know how the other half live. The wife likes all that stuff, but for me, not much beats sitting on a bench by the river in Bakewell stuffing my face with fish and chips followed by a cup of tea and a brief encounter with a Bakewell Tart!

Treasure Hunting

Purchasing a metal detector won't cost a fortune and could give you much fun. At the very least you'll get plenty of fresh air and exercise, but you might unearth a pirates treasure!

Beachcombing can also be great even just for some of the driftwood. One of our sons collects driftwood and combines it with stain glass to produce some brilliant creative wall hangings and tea lights.

And collecting certain pebbles and shells can also be fun and turned into creative art. But if you find a shell on the beach with suspicious markings like: "Made in Germany 1939", don't hit it with your shovel - run like shit! - Preferably away from the sea!

Or how about panning for gold? Apparently the rivers and brooks in Wales are full of the stuff. There are people who do this as a full time occupation, but it can also be just a bit of fun!

Miniature Sailing

While we lived in Lincolnshire we'd often go to Cleethorpes where there's a really nice park with a couple of lakes at the

South end of the promenade. Regularly on a Sunday morning you'll find a group of oldies racing their remote controlled sailing boats on one of these lakes - what a brilliant thing to do! If we still lived there, I'd be one of them!

Drama Groups

Drama Groups are active in all areas and if you are interested, there's no doubt that you will be welcome, as all ages are needed for this activity. Even if you feel unable to take part in the acting, there are many activities behind the scenes where your help would no doubt be most welcomed.

Learn a Musical Instrument

Learning a musical instrument can enrich your retirement beyond belief and you are never too old to learn. Personally I play keyboards and once toured as a professional. Now I write music and music instruction books as well as amusing myself and annoying the wife!

Buying a starter keyboard needn't be expensive at all, especially if purchased second-hand. Some of the low cost Casios and Yamahas are remarkably good for the money and even if you don't progress very far, can give endless enjoyment. See my site: http://gonkmusic.com for some low cost complete keyboard tuition books and don't forget to ask me for an OAP discount!

But even if you think that you are totally incapable of learning a musical instrument, why not try a pair of bongos. You'd be amazed at how much fun you can have playing around with a pair of bongos! - Or a single djembe drum. These require no musical training as such, just rhythm - which we've all got, and can give you hours of pleasure and fulfilment. They could also piss your neighbours off beyond belief - but you could go out into the local park and annoy the pigeons. And you might even make a few bob if you leave your hat the right way up!

Help Others

Helping others as a volunteer can give you an enriching purpose in life as well as the good you may do. No doubt your local church will point you in the right direction.

Socialise with Friends

One of the really enriching things about living in Cyprus was the fact that ex pats would get together and socialise far more so than we seem to at home. And the rich / poor barrier seemed to vanish.

Just about every day, we would go to see someone or others would come to see us, just for a cup of tea etc., but it was great!

Most of the friends we made in Cyprus have also come back to Blighty and we still see them, although not so often as they are widely spread across Britain.

But engaging in any of the activities mentioned already will also open up the potential for your social life to be enriched.

So I think you'll agree that there's an awful lot of stuff that you can do that won't cost you a fortune if anything at all. And here we've only scraped the surface!

Loneliness

If all the lonely people in the world got together, they couldn't possibly be lonely! This is another good reason to get computer savvy as Skype could enable you to keep in touch with friends and relatives even hundreds or thousands of miles away for virtually no cost without even getting out of your Shackletons.

But of course, the above could only deal with a bit of the problem. When all your friends have snuffed it and you've gone gaga, it can be a real problem which many of us may face one day.

Recent surveys have concluded that many people don't even know who's living next door to them - frightening! If you live in a semi and start playing with your bongos in the early hours, I absolutely guarantee that you'll soon get to meet them! In fact if you do it in the garden you'll meet the whole street!

But seriously, we're all becoming gradually more vulnerable, but while you've still got a full set of marbles it's a great idea to help anyone locally who may be lonely and have no-one. In many cases this may only entail nipping round for a quick cup of tea (which may well make their day) or seeing if they need anything fetching from the shops. Just a friendly presence can make such a difference to many.

And while you're at it make sure that they are receiving their correct financial entitlements, which can be a tricky problem as they probably won't want to talk about it. But if you can see that their home is cold and there's no food in the cupboards, clearly something is wrong and they need help.

If you are affected by loneliness or know anyone who is, a great contact is good old Ester Rantzen's new 24 hour helpline for older people at: http://www.thesilverline.org.uk - Tel: 0800 4 70 80 90. You can help this fantastic cause by donating, volunteering, or taking part in sporting events etc.

Pets

Having a pet can enrich your life without a doubt, but if you haven't already got one consider carefully which type would be best for you.

You need to consider the costs involved and the needs of the animal. For instance if you have limited walking capabilities, having a large dog that will require a lot of exercise will not be a good idea. Whereas a cat which will require little effort on your part may be a better option. But could you cope with a frolicsome kitten crawling up you curtains etc.?

Walking the right sized dog for your capabilities could give you exercise as well as getting to meet other dog owners.

Goldfish can also give great pleasure as they are very calming to watch although I doubt that you could have a meaningful interaction with one.

Another excellent choice could be a parrot, which are cheap to feed and can be great company as they are very interactive. They can also live a long time - *if you don't have a cat as well!*

Other things to consider are:

- Vet costs and general inoculations etc.;
- Food and other costs - diamond encrusted collars etc.;
- Kennel fees;
- The eventual pain of losing them.

Personally we have a Bengali cat called Kizzie who is the love of our lives. In her eyes the wife and I are just servants who are there to cater for her every whim. Fortunately when she wants feeding in the middle of the night she wakes the wife up and not me, so she's got that one right!

I'm not sure whether I am No. 2 or 3 in the pecking order, but she's definitely *numero uno!*

Conclusion

Well folks that's nearly all. Hopefully you've gained some valuable information herein. To be honest, I've learnt an awful lot myself whilst writing this, some of which has really surprised me.

Here's a recap:

- Check your income and savings to see if you are eligible for the *guaranteed* pension credit. And if the only thing that is preventing you from becoming eligible is your savings, then consider spending some particularly on items that may improve your lifestyle or future fuel bills;

- If you are not eligible for the *guaranteed* credit, you may still be entitled to the *savings* element (even if you own your own house but don't have any savings) AND a proportion of your council tax payments - YOU MUST CHECK THIS;

- Become computer savvy and live in the present century - we live in an ever changing world - resign yourself to it!;

- Shop wisely - take a list and don't impulse buy unless it's a BOGOF or better for item(s) that you need and can save (not perishable);

- Keep a contingency fund;

- Keep a keen eye out for usable vouchers and coupons;

- Budget correctly and always be aware of all of your outgoings;

- Shop around for the best utility and insurance prices every year - remember your loyalty won't be rewarded;

- After researching the best prices, use Quidco or Topcashback wherever you can to make extra savings;

- If you have a car, be aware of your cost per mile (including running costs) and don't use it for short or unnecessary journeys - consider National Travel and rail deals as an alternative;

- Take full advantage of your bus pass;

- Consider Equity Release to either gain capital or to move to a more expensive property, but remember it could affect pension credits (either way);

- Consider downsizing to a more eco property;

- Look into telephone / broadband arrangements that best suit your needs and budget;

- Use banks and credit cards to *your* advantage not theirs;

- If you need to choose between *heating* or *eating* then you are either mismanaging your affairs badly or not receiving the benefits to which you are entitled;

- Deal with debts without delay, but only seek guidance from a reliable source such as National Debt line or Citizens Advice Bureau (see resources);

- Insure against disaster (at the right price), but weigh up the odds on everything else;

- Install a water butt and other water saving devices;

- Re-discover all the things you can do for free;

- Only consider safe investments with the highest yields and / or change to the best ISA etc.;

- Be ever vigilant for fraudsters both online and off - they could be offering to fix your roof or sell you a dodgy investment and they come in all shapes and sizes!

And finally, just a couple of words of warning:

- If your kids offer to take you on a nice short break to Switzerland, make sure that you see the return ticket;

- Always be on your guard and remember that the next fart could be a wet one!; and

- Remember to hang onto your nuts when you take your last breath (I'm not sure what the lady's need to hang onto).

And when that last breath finally comes, fear not, it's not game over, you just go into a cocoon for a while and then re-emerge as a beautiful butterfly! A bit like moving onto the next level with a new set of balls!

That sounds nice, but how can you be sure of this?

The wife told me - remember she knows everything!

Disclaimer

The information in this book has been written with the best of intentions and to my knowledge is correct at the time of writing, but as laws and benefits etc. are altering all the time, no responsibility can be accepted for any inaccuracies herein.

You are advised to seek independent legal advice before considering any financial commitments.

In April of each year, the basic state pension increases along with the pension credit figures. I shall consequently be updating my online calculations on an annual basis as these figures become available.

Unless you have an index linked private pension in real terms you will become less well off as the years go by, so keep checking your eligibility to claim pension credit!

Last But Not Least

Last but by no means least - ***thank you sincerely*** for trusting me enough to buy this book. It's always my aim to offer more in use value than I receive in payment. I hope I've succeeded.

If you've enjoyed this and found it useful, *your positive feedback from wherever you made your purchase would be gratefully appreciated*.

Thanks again - Martin.

Resources

Below is a list of useful resource links. Note that I have not received any payment for including any of these here, and neither would I if offered. So you can be sure that they have been chosen with *your best interest in mind only* and not theirs. But this does not mean that I necessarily particularly recommend any of them.

With the exception of the first few which I consider to be the most important, they are listed alphabetically. The ones marked with the ** I consider to be particularly important or useful.

Pension Credit Information

To find out if you may be eligible for the guaranteed credit go to: http://martinwoodward.net/pen.html **

http://www.ageuk.org.uk/pension-credit **

https://www.gov.uk/pension-credit ** Tel: 0800 991 234 (Monday to Friday from 8.00am to 6.00pm) - Textphone: 0800 169 0133

Warm Home Discount Scheme

https://www.gov.uk/the-warm-home-discount-scheme **

http://www.boilergrants.info **

Age UK guide to More Money in Your Pocket

http://www.ageuk.org.uk/Documents **

My Budget and mpg Calculators

http://martinwoodward.net/pen1.html **

http://martinwoodward.net/pen2.html **

Motability

http://www.motability.co.uk **

Martin Lewis Money Saving Expert

http://www.moneysavingexpert.com **

Budgeting Software (free)

http://www.codelathe.com/mmex **

http://homebank.free.fr **

http://www.gnucash.org **

Buy to Let on a Budget

http://martinwoodward.net/buy_to_let.html **

http://martinwoodward.net/cyprus.html *- free* **

Cashback Sites

http://www.quidco.com **

http://www.topcashback.co.uk **

http://www.vouchercodes.com **

Central Heating Cover

http://www.britishgas.co.uk

Contactless Credit / Debit Card Info

http://www.visa.co.uk/contactless **

Crime Rates

http://www.police.uk **

Debt Help

http://www.stepchange.org **

https://www.gov.uk/bankruptcy **

https://www.moneyadviceservice.org.uk **

https://www.moneyadviceservice.org.uk/en **

Electric Heating
http://sunflowltd.co.uk

http://www.fischer-futureheat.co.uk

Equity Release
http://www.keyrs.co.uk/equity-release **

http://www.agepartnership.co.uk

Holiday Insurance
http://www.staysure.co.uk/home **

http://www.nhs-e111-ehic.org.uk **

Insurance Info and comparison sites
http://www.moneysupermarket.com **

http://www.directline.com/home-insurance

http://www.gocompare.com/insurance **

http://www.confused.com/insurance **

http://www.comparethemarket.com

Internet Security
https://www.trusteer.com/products/trusteer-rapport **

Microsoft Security Essentials free antivirus download
http://www.microsoft.com **

Malwarebytes - free antimalware software
https://www.malwarebytes.org

Lavasoft - free antimalware software
http://www.lavasoft.com

Spybot - free antimalware software
http://www.safer-networking.org **

Light Bulb Info
http://eartheasy.com/live_energyeff_lighting.htm **

http://www.designrecycleinc.com

Loneliness
Ester Rantzen's - Silver Line Helpline for Older People

http://www.thesilverline.org.uk ** - **0800 4 70 80 90**

Loyalty Cards
http://www.tesco.com/clubcard

http://www.nectar.com

http://www.co-operative.coop/membership

http://www.boots.com/en/Advantage-Card

http://www.johnlewis.com **

https://www.waitrose.com **

http://www.energyplusargos.co.uk

Mobile Internet & Phone Providers
http://www.three.co.uk/Store/Mobile_Broadband **

http://www.vodafone.co.uk

http://www.lycamobile.co.uk **

http://giffgaff.com **

http://shop.orange.co.uk

https://corp.fon.com/en **

http://www.togglemobile.co.uk/home/en (for UK & European mobile phone) **

http://www.europasim.com/en_GB (for European internet)

http://www.sambamobile.com/Home/Samba (was free but currently not available)

http://www.motorhomewifi.com (ideal for travellers)

Motoring

MPG calculator and cost of trip calculator (free)
http://martinwoodward.net/pen2.html **

Accident report form (free) - handy to keep in your glove box
- http://martinwoodward.net/accident_form **

http://www.autoaidbreakdown.co.uk **

http://www.bangernomics.com

http://www.jamesruppert.com/bangernomics-bible.html

Music Tuition

http://gonkmusic.com **

OAP Discounts

http://www.partnersplumbers.co.uk/discounts

http://www.seniorsdiscounts.co.uk

http://www.senior-railcard.co.uk **

http://www.myvue.com/offers-savings/senior-vue

http://www.nationalexpress.com/senior **

http://www.thetrainline.com **

http://www.taybarns.com/taybarns.html

http://travelsouthyorkshire.com

Online Auction and Selling Sites

http://www.ebay.co.uk

https://www.amazon.co.uk

http://www.gumtree.com

http://www.vivastreet.co.uk

http://uk.ebid.net

http://www.preloved.co.uk

https://www.etsy.com **

Online Data Storage
https://skydrive.live.com **

https://drive.google.com **

Online Data Storage cont...
http://photobucket.com

http://www.snapfish.com

Online Newspapers
http://www.wrx.zen.co.uk **

Pets
http://www.pdsa.org.uk

http://www.animalfriends.org.uk

Radiator Reflectors
http://www.heatkeeper.co.uk **

Radon Gas
http://www.ukradon.org **

Relaxation CD's
http://deep-relaxation.co.uk**

Restaurants with Great Discounts
https://www.brewersfayrebonusclub.co.uk

http://www.damons.co.uk

http://www.taybarns.com **

http://www.oldharrow.co.uk**

http://www.flaming-dragon.co.uk**

http://www.jdwetherspoon.co.uk (currently no OAP discounts but possibly in the future)

Sale of Goods Act

http://www.which.co.uk/consumer-rights/regulation/sale-of-goods-act

Say No to 0870

http://www.saynoto0870.com/ **

Skill Swap Sites

http://www.skillbound.com

http://www.localskillswap.com

http://www.gumtree.com

Skype

http://www.skype.com/en **

Smart Phone Information

Which guide to smart phones 0800 533 000

http://www.which.co.uk/phones

Solar Panels & Wind Turbines

http://www.solarquotes.co.uk **

http://www.solarpanelquoter.co.uk

http://www.enviko.com

http://www.which.co.uk/energy

http://www.which.co.uk/energy/solar-panels

Supermarkets Online

http://www.mysupermarket.co.uk **

http://www.tesco.com/groceries

https://www.waitrose.com

http://www.asda.com

http://www.sainsburys.co.uk

Supermarkets Online cont...

http://www.morrisons.com

https://www.aldi.co.uk

http://www.lidl.co.uk

http://www.co-operativefood.co.uk

http://www.iceland.co.uk

http://www.farmfoods.co.uk

http://www.fultonsfoods.co.uk

http://www.spar.co.uk

http://www.budgens.co.uk

Telephone Preference Service

http://www.callpreventionregistry.co.uk **

Tel: 0800 652 7780

Travel

http://www.redspottedhanky.com

http://www.senior-railcard.co.uk **

http://www.nationalexpress.com **

http://www.thetrainline.com **

http://www.freebustravel.co.uk**

http://www.eastcoast.co.uk

University for the 3rd Age

http://www.u3a.org.uk **

Utility Info & Comparison sites

http://www.energyhelpline.com

http://www.uswitch.com

http://www.moneysupermarket.com **

Westfield Health Scheme
http://www.westfieldhealth.com **

Tel: 0114 250 2000

Which Guide to State Pensions
http://www.which.co.uk/money/retirement

White Good Insurance
http://www.domgen.com

Window Security
http://www.jackloc.com **

0800 Call Buster
http://www.0800buster.co.uk **

And Here's a few Freebies from the Public Domain:
The Ancient Secret of the Fountain of Youth -
http://www.lib.ru/URIKOVA/KELDER/Ancient_Secret_of_the_Fountain_of_Youth-Peter_Kelder.pdf

The Science of Getting Rich - Wallace Wattles
http://martinwoodward.net/030412wattlegettingrich.pdf

The Magic of Believing - Claude M Bristol -
http://www.tedleithart.com//The-Magic-of-Believing-by-Claude-Bristol.pdf

The Richest Man in Babylon -
http://www.ccsales.com/the_richest_man_in_babylon.pdf

You may also like:

http://martinwoodward.net

http://gonkmusic.com

http://deep-relaxation.co.uk/golden_sphere.html

www.ingramcontent.com/pod-product-compliance
Lightning Source LLC
Chambersburg PA
CBHW021959170526
45157CB00003B/1064